KITCHEN
TABLE

100 Sweet Treats and Puds

KITCHEN TABLE gives you a wealth of recipes from your favourite chefs. Whether you want a quick weekday supper, sumptuous weekend feast or food for friends and family, let the My Kitchen Table experts bring their favourite dishes to your home.

To get exclusive recipes, read our blog, subscribe to our newsletter or find out the latest on our exciting My Kitchen Table recipe App, visit www.mykitchentable.co.uk

Throughout this book, when you see my KITCHEN TABLE visit our site for practical videos, tips and hints from the My Kitchen Table team.

**KITCHEN
TABLE**

100 Sweet Treats and Puds
MARY BERRY

www.mykitchentable.co.uk

Welcome to MY KITCHEN TABLE

Go on, treat yourself to a homemade sweet bake. Whether it be for teatime, a mid-morning snack or for dessert, take inspiration from the **100 foolproof and delicious sugary recipes** selected here.

Contents

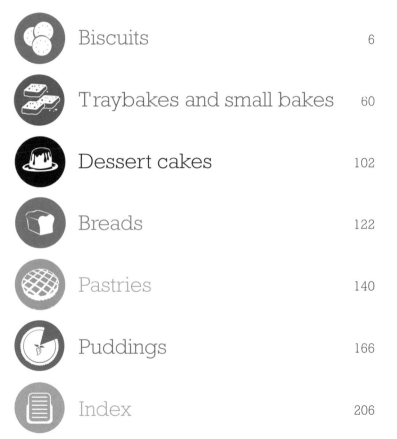

Fork Biscuits

These biscuits first made their appearance in an old red *Cordon Bleu* cookery book, and I've been making them for years.

Step one Preheat the oven to 180°C/fan 160°C/gas 4. Lightly butter the baking trays.

Step two Measure the butter into a bowl and beat to soften. Gradually beat in the sugar and then the flour. Bring the mixture together with your hands to form a dough. Form the dough into 16 balls about the size of a walnut and place spaced well apart on the prepared baking trays. Dip a fork in a little water and use this to flatten the biscuits.

Step three Bake in the preheated oven for 15–20 minutes until a very pale golden. Lift off the baking tray and leave to cool completely on a wire rack.

To make Chocolate Fork Biscuits, follow the recipe above, but use only 120g (4½oz) self-raising flour along with 15g (½oz) cocoa powder. Bake until browned.

To make Orange or Lemon Fork Biscuits, follow the recipe above but add the grated zest of 1 small orange or lemon when you beat in the caster sugar. Bake until very pale golden.

Makes 16

Equipment needed:
2 baking trays

100g (4oz) butter, softened

50g (2oz) caster sugar

150g (5oz) self-raising flour

Shrewsbury Biscuits

These biscuits have a delicate lemony flavour.

Makes 24

Equipment needed:
3 baking trays

100g (4oz) butter,
softened

75g (3oz) caster sugar

1 large egg, separated

200g (7oz) plain flour

grated zest of 1 lemon

50g (2oz) currants

1–2 tbsp milk

caster sugar,
for sprinkling

Step one Preheat the oven to 200°C/fan 180°C/gas 6. Lightly butter the baking trays.

Step two Measure the butter and sugar into a bowl and cream together until light and fluffy. Beat in the egg yolk. Sift in the flour, add the grated lemon zest and mix well. Add the currants and enough milk to give a fairly soft dough.

Step three Knead the mixture gently on a lightly floured surface and roll out to a thickness of 5mm (¼in). Cut into about 24 rounds using a 6cm (2½in) fluted cutter. Place on the prepared baking trays.

Step four Bake in the preheated oven for 8–10 minutes. Meanwhile, lightly beat the egg whites. Remove the biscuits from the oven, brush with beaten egg white, sprinkle with a little caster sugar and return to the oven for a further 4–5 minutes or until pale golden brown. Lift onto a wire rack to cool and then store in an airtight container.

KITCHEN
TABLE

For more recipes from My Kitchen Table, sign up for our newsletter at
www.mykitchentable.co.uk/newsletter

Chocolate Chip Cookies

Don't expect these cookies to be as crisp as traditional biscuits – they should be slightly chewy. For a change, you could chop a bar of plain orange chocolate into small cubes and use instead of the chocolate chips. The cookies will keep in a tin for a week.

Step one Preheat the oven to 190°C/fan 170°C/gas 5. Lightly butter the baking trays.

Step two Measure the butter and sugars into a medium-sized bowl and beat thoroughly until evenly blended. Add the vanilla extract to the beaten egg and then add a little at a time to the butter and sugar mixture in the bowl, beating well between each addition. Mix in the flour, and lastly stir in the chocolate chips. Spoon large teaspoons of the mixture onto the prepared baking trays, leaving room for the cookies to spread.

Step three Bake the cookies in batches in the preheated oven, on the top shelf, for 8–10 minutes or until the cookies are golden. Watch them like a hawk, as they will turn dark brown very quickly. Leave the cookies to cool on the trays for a few minutes, then lift off with a palette knife or fish slice and place on a wire cooling rack. Leave to cool completely, then store in an airtight tin.

Makes 20

Equipment needed:
3 baking trays

100g (4oz) butter, softened

75g (3oz) caster sugar

50g (2oz) light muscovado sugar

½ tsp vanilla extract

1 large egg, beaten

150g (5oz) self-raising flour

100g (4oz) plain chocolate chips

Lime Lattice Cookies

Use the juice of the limes in drinks, or to add a lovely flavour to whipped cream.

Makes 16

Equipment needed:
2 baking trays

100g (4oz) butter,
softened

50g (2oz) caster sugar

150g (5oz)
self-raising flour

finely grated zest
of 2 limes

Step one Preheat the oven to 180°C/fan 160°C/gas 4. Lightly butter the baking trays.

Step two Measure the butter and sugar into a bowl and beat together to a creamy consistency. Add the flour and grated lime zest. Bring the mixture together to form a dough. Form the dough into 16 balls the size of a walnut and place on the prepared baking trays. Flatten the balls slightly and then use a skewer to create a lattice pattern in the top of the biscuits.

Step three Bake in the preheated oven for 10–15 minutes or until just beginning to turn golden. Lift onto a wire rack and leave to cool.

Double Chocolate Cookies

Dead easy to make, these are wonderful cookies. Expect an irregular shape. They are very soft when they come out of the oven but will harden up considerably on cooling.

Step one Lightly butter the baking trays. Break up the chocolate and gently melt it along with the butter in a heatproof bowl set over a pan of barely simmering water or in a microwave, taking care not to burn the chocolate, stirring occasionally. Stir in the condensed milk, then remove from the heat and cool.

Step two Mix in the flour and the chocolate buttons and chill the mixture until firm enough to handle. Preheat the oven to 180°C/fan 160°C/gas 4.

Step three Place large teaspoonfuls of the mixture spaced well apart on the prepared baking trays. Bake in the preheated oven for about 15 minutes. The cookies should still look soft and will glisten. Don't overcook them, as they soon become very hard. Carefully remove the cookies with a palette knife and cool on a wire rack.

Makes 36

Equipment needed:
3 baking trays

200g (7oz) plain chocolate (39 per cent cocoa solids)

50g (2oz) butter

1 x 397g (14oz) tin full fat condensed milk

225g (8oz) self-raising flour

65g (2½ oz) milk or white chocolate buttons

Melting Moments

These old-fashioned biscuits are very short in texture. They are best eaten within a couple of days of making.

Makes 36

Equipment needed:
2 baking trays

225g (8oz) butter, softened

175g (6oz) golden caster sugar

2 large egg yolks

a few drops vanilla extract

275g (10oz) self-raising flour

50g (2oz) porridge oats

9 red or natural glacé cherries, quartered (optional)

Step one Preheat the oven to 190°C/fan 170°C/gas 5. Line the baking trays with non-stick baking parchment.

Step two Measure the butter, sugar, egg yolks, vanilla extract and flour into a mixing bowl and beat together to form a soft dough.

Step three Divide the mixture into about 36 portions. Form each piece into a ball and roll in the oats to cover. Flatten each ball slightly and top each with a quartered glacé cherry, if you like. Place on the prepared baking trays.

Step four Bake in the preheated oven for about 20 minutes or until golden. Allow to cool slightly on the baking trays for a few minutes before lifting onto a wire rack to cool.

Bishop's Fingers

If you notice that the underside of the shortbread is not pale golden, return the tin to the oven for a further 5–10 minutes.

Step one Preheat the oven to 160°C/fan 140°C/gas 3. Lightly butter the tin.

Step two Mix together the flour, ground almonds and semolina in a bowl or food processor. Add the butter, sugar and almond extract and rub together with your fingertips until the mixture is just beginning to bind together. Knead lightly until smooth. Press the dough into the prepared tin and level the surface with the back of a metal spoon or a palette knife. Sprinkle over the flaked almonds.

Step three Bake in the preheated oven for 30–35 minutes or until a very pale golden brown. Mark the shortbread into 12 fingers with a knife, sprinkle with caster sugar and leave to cool in the tin. When completely cold, cut into fingers, lift out carefully and store in an airtight tin.

Makes 12

Cake tin needed:
an 18cm (7in) shallow
square tin

100g (4oz) plain flour

25g (1oz)
ground almonds

25g (1oz) semolina

100g (4oz) butter

50g (2oz) caster sugar

a few drops
almond extract

25g (1oz) flaked
almonds

caster sugar,
for dusting

Cheese Straws

These make a lovely gift presented in a box. You can make them in advance, but keep them in the fridge and not the larder as they can quickly become stale. Freeze them once cold – they taste good even when freezer-hard.

Makes 30

Equipment needed:
2 baking trays

100g (4oz) plain flour

75g (3oz) butter, softened

50g (2oz) grated mature Cheddar

1 large egg yolk

finely grated Parmesan, for sprinkling

Step one Measure the flour into a bowl and rub in the butter with your fingertips until the mixture resembles fine breadcrumbs. Stir in the grated Cheddar. Reserve a tiny bit of the egg yolk for glazing and stir in the remainder. Bring the mixture together to form a dough. Wrap in clingfilm and chill in the fridge for about 30 minutes.

Step two When the dough has chilled, preheat the oven to 190°C/fan 170°C/gas 5 and lightly butter the baking trays. Roll the chilled dough out on a lightly floured work surface to a thickness of about 5mm (¼in). Cut into neat strips about 5mm (¼in) wide and about 10cm (4in) long. Place on the prepared baking trays, brush with the remaining egg yolk and sprinkle generously with grated Parmesan.

Step three Bake in the preheated oven for 10–15 minutes or until golden. Lift off the baking trays and leave to cool completely on a wire rack. Pack carefully in baking parchment in a gift box and give as fresh as possible, or freeze until ready to offer.

Cornish Fairings

Take care not to bake these spicy biscuits too long as they become hard and too crisp. Banging the baking tray part of the way through cooking makes the mixture crack and flatten.

Step one Preheat the oven to 180°C/fan 160°C/gas 4. Lightly butter the baking trays.

Step two Measure the flour, spices and bicarbonate of soda into a bowl. Rub the butter into the flour with your fingertips until the mixture resembles fine breadcrumbs, then mix in the sugar.

Step three Gently heat the golden syrup and stir into the mixture to make a soft dough. Roll the dough into 24 balls roughly about the size of a cherry and place on the prepared baking trays, allowing room for them to spread.

Step four Bake in the preheated oven for about 10 minutes, then take the baking trays out of the oven and carefully hit on a solid surface to make the biscuits crack and spread. Bake for a further 5 minutes until they are a good even brown. Lift off the baking trays and leave to cool on a wire rack.

Makes 24

Equipment needed:
2 baking trays

100g (4oz) plain flour

¼ level tsp
ground ginger

¼ level tsp ground
mixed spice

¼ level tsp
ground cinnamon

½ level tsp
bicarbonate of soda

50g (2oz) butter,
softened

50g (2oz) caster sugar

75g (3oz)
golden syrup

Dorchester Biscuits

Savoury biscuits are great to go with drinks and these cheesey, nutty ones are delicious. Children like to roll these little balls, and they could give them as a present to a relative.

Makes 30

Equipment needed:
2 baking trays

100g (4oz) mature Cheddar, grated

100g (4oz) plain flour

a little salt

100g (4oz) butter, softened

¼ tsp cayenne pepper

50g (2oz) finely chopped unsalted mixed nuts, plus a few more for sprinkling

Step one Preheat the oven to 180°C/fan 160°C/gas 4. Lightly butter the baking trays.

Step two Measure all the ingredients, except the nuts for sprinkling, into a bowl and work together with a knife and then your hand to form a dough. Form the dough into 30 balls about the size of a walnut and place spaced well apart on the prepared baking trays.

Step three Sprinkle with finely chopped mixed nuts and then just lightly flatten the balls with your hand. Bake in the preheated oven for about 15–20 minutes or until golden brown. Lift onto a wire rack to cool. Serve warm or cold.

Try whole or halved cashew nuts for the topping, instead of the chopped nuts.

Lavender Biscuits

Both the flowers and the leaves of lavender can be used, although it is best to use young leaves. If you are using fresh lavender, make sure it is unsprayed. Dried lavender is stronger in flavour, so use half the quantity.

Step one Lightly butter the baking trays. Put the softened butter and the lavender into a mixing bowl and beat together. This will extract the maximum flavour from the lavender.

Step two Beat the caster sugar into the butter and lavender and then stir in the flour, bringing the mixture together with your hands and kneading lightly until smooth.

Step three Divide the mixture in half and roll out to form two sausage shapes 15cm (6in) long. Roll the biscuit 'sausages' in the demerara sugar until evenly coated. Wrap in non-stick baking parchment or foil and chill until firm.

Step four Preheat the oven to 160°C/fan 140°C/gas 3. Cut each 'sausage' into about 10 slices and put them on the prepared baking trays, allowing a little room for them to spread. Bake in the preheated oven for 15–20 minutes, until the biscuits are pale golden brown at the edges. Lift them off the trays with a fish slice or palette knife and place on a wire rack. Sprinkle with extra lavender flowers to decorate, if using, and leave to cool completely.

Makes 20

Equipment needed:
3 large baking trays

175g (6oz) unsalted butter, softened

2 level tbsp fresh, unsprayed, finely chopped lavender flowers and leaves (pick the flowerlets and the leaves off the stems to measure), or 1 level tbsp dried lavender, plus extra, to decorate (optional)

100g (4oz) caster sugar

225g (8oz) plain flour

25g (1oz) demerara sugar

Yorkshire Gingernuts

Very quick to make and deliciously crunchy, these biscuits look nice stored in an attractive glass jar.

Makes 50

Equipment needed:
3 baking trays

100g (4oz) butter

1 generous tbsp
golden syrup

350g (12oz)
self-raising flour

100g (4oz)
demerara sugar

100g (4oz) light
muscovado sugar

1 level tsp
bicarbonate of soda

1 level tbsp
ground ginger

1 large egg, beaten

Step one Preheat the oven to 160°C/fan 140°C/gas 3. Lightly butter the baking trays.

Step two Measure the butter and golden syrup into a small pan and gently heat together until the butter has melted. Mix all the dry ingredients together in a large bowl, then add the melted butter mixture and the egg to form a dough.

Step three Form the dough into 50 balls about the size of a walnut and place spaced well apart on the prepared baking trays.

Step four Bake in the preheated oven for 15–20 minutes or until golden. Lift off the baking trays and leave to cool on a wire rack.

Oat Rounds

These biscuits are first cousin to the digestive biscuit, with added oats. They are good with cheese or jam, or eaten by themselves with morning coffee, and have become a firm favourite in our house.

Step one Preheat the oven to 160°C/fan 140°C/gas 3. Lightly butter the baking trays.

Step two Measure the sugar and butter into a bowl and beat together to a creamy consistency. Add the oats and flour and work them into the mixture. Lightly knead the mixture until smooth and then roll out to a thickness of 5mm (¼in) on a lightly floured work surface.

Step three Cut into 16 rounds using a 6cm (2½in) plain cutter and place on the prepared baking trays. Bake in the preheated oven for about 20 minutes or until beginning to turn golden. Lift onto a wire rack to cool.

Makes 16

Equipment needed:
2 baking trays

50g (2oz) caster sugar

100g (4oz) butter, softened

100g (4oz) porridge oats

50g (2oz) plain flour

Viennese Fingers

These biscuits must be made with butter. The mixture holds its shape
beautifully for piping, so use it for any style of piped biscuit.

Makes 20

Equipment needed:
2 baking trays

100g (4oz) butter,
softened

25g (1oz) icing sugar

100g (4oz) plain flour

¼ level tsp
baking powder

50g (2oz) plain
chocolate (39 per
cent cocoa solids)

Step one Preheat the oven to 190°C/fan 170°C/gas 5.
Lightly butter the baking trays. Fit a piping bag with a
medium star nozzle.

Step two Measure the butter and icing sugar into a bowl
and beat well until pale and fluffy. Sift in the flour and baking
powder. Beat well until thoroughly mixed. Spoon into the
piping bag and pipe out finger shapes about 7.5cm (3in)
long, spacing them well apart on the baking trays.

Step three Bake in the preheated oven for 10–15 minutes
or until a pale golden brown. Lift off and cool on a wire rack.

Step four Break the chocolate into pieces and melt it in a
heatproof bowl set over a pan of barely simmering water or in
a microwave, stirring occasionally, and taking care not to burn
the chocolate. Dip both ends of the biscuits into the chocolate
and leave to set on the wire rack.

*To fill a piping bag, stand the bag with the nozzle pointing
down into a jug and then fold the top edges of the bag over
the top of the jug. That way, it is much easier to spoon the
mixture (or meringue, whipped cream or icing) into the
bag without getting it all over yourself.*

Florentines

Using non-stick baking parchment makes it so much simpler to get these biscuits off the baking trays. You can simply use well-buttered baking trays, but be careful not to leave the Florentines for too long or they will harden before you have a chance to lift them off.

Step one Preheat the oven to 180°C/fan 160°C/gas 4. Line the baking trays with non-stick baking parchment.

Step two Measure the butter, sugar and syrup into a small pan and heat gently until the butter has melted. Remove from the heat and add the flour, chopped cherries, candied peel and nuts to the pan and stir well to mix. Spoon teaspoonfuls of the mixture onto the prepared baking trays, leaving plenty of room for them to spread.

Step three Bake in the preheated oven for 8–10 minutes or until golden brown. Leave the Florentines to cool before lifting onto a cooling rack with a palette knife (if the Florentines have been baked on buttered baking trays, only allow them to harden for a few moments before lifting onto wire racks to cool completely). If the Florentines become too hard to remove, put them back into the oven for a few moments to allow them to soften.

Step four Break the chocolate into pieces and melt it in a heatproof bowl set over a pan of barely simmering water or in a microwave, stirring occasionally, and taking care not to burn the chocolate. Spread a little melted chocolate over the flat base of each Florentine using a palette knife, and leave to set, chocolate-side up, on the cooling rack. Store in an airtight container.

These are luxurious biscuits, but you do need patience and accurate scales to make them.

Makes 20

Equipment needed:
3 baking trays

50g (2oz) butter

50g (2oz)
demerara sugar

50g (2oz)
golden syrup

50g (2oz) plain flour

4 red or natural
glacé cherries,
finely chopped

50g (2oz) finely
chopped candied peel

50g (2oz) finely
chopped mixed
almonds and walnuts

175g (6oz) plain
chocolate (39 per
cent cocoa solids)

Petits Fours aux Amandes

These make a very special present – petits fours tend to be rather fiddly to make for oneself! Look out for a pretty or unusual plate in an antique shop or car boot sale, and arrange the petits fours on this. Cover with clear cellophane and decorate with a ribbon. The milk and sugar glaze is optional for these petits fours, but it does give a nice shine.

Makes 24

Equipment needed:
2 baking trays

2 large egg whites

100g (4oz)
ground almonds

75g (3oz) caster sugar

a few drops
almond extract

red or natural glacé
cherries, chopped, to
decorate

to finish

1 level tbsp
caster sugar

2 tbsp milk

Step one Preheat the oven to 180°C/fan 160°C/gas 4. Line the baking trays with non-stick baking parchment. Fit a piping bag with a large star nozzle.

Step two Whisk the egg whites until stiff. Fold in the ground almonds, sugar and almond extract. Spoon the mixture into the prepared piping bag and pipe the mixture into small rosettes onto the prepared baking trays. Decorate each rosette with a small piece of glacé cherry.

Step three Bake in the preheated oven for about 15 minutes or until golden. Lift onto a wire rack. To finish, mix the caster sugar and milk together and lightly brush over the petits fours.

Chocolate Ganache Petits Fours

These are irresistible, but keep them in a cool place or they'll become very soft.

Step one First, make the chocolate casings. Break the chocolate into pieces and heat gently along with the oil in a heatproof bowl set over a pan of barely simmering water or in a microwave, stirring occasionally until the chocolate has melted, taking care not to burn the chocolate.

Step two Allow to cool slightly, then brush the inside of about 24 paper petits fours cases with a thin layer of chocolate (you can use a fine brush to do this, or even just your fingertip). Leave to set in a cool place. Give the cases a second coat of chocolate and again leave to set.

Step three To make the ganache, break the chocolate into pieces. Pour the cream into a small saucepan and bring to the boil. Remove from the heat and add the chocolate pieces and a little rum or brandy. Stir until the chocolate has melted.

Step four Return the pan to the heat, bring to the boil and then take off the heat and leave to cool. When firm, spoon the chocolate ganache into a piping bag fitted with a medium star nozzle and pipe rosettes of the ganache into the chocolate cases.

Step five Carefully peel off the paper cases. Decorate the top of each petit four with a pistachio nut, and keep in a cool place until required.

Makes 24

Equipment needed: about 24 petits fours cases

for the casings

175g (6oz) plain chocolate (39 per cent cocoa solids)

1 tsp sunflower oil

for the chocolate ganache filling

100g (4oz) plain chocolate (39 per cent cocoa solids)

150ml (¼ pint) double cream (not extra thick)

rum or brandy, to flavour

to decorate

shelled pistachio nuts

Have you made this recipe? Tell us what you think at www.mykitchentable.co.uk/blog

Muesli Cookies

The flavour and consistency will depend on the muesli used. These are good for a lunch box, for a snack at school or work, or to take on a picnic.

Makes 28

Equipment needed:
3 baking trays

175g (6oz) butter, softened

100g (4oz) caster sugar

1 large egg

175g (6oz) self-raising flour

175g (6oz) muesli, plus a little extra for sprinkling

demerara sugar, for sprinkling

Step one Preheat the oven to 180°C/fan 160°C/gas 4. Lightly butter the baking trays.

Step two Measure all the ingredients, except the muesli and the demerara sugar, into a large bowl and beat together until well blended and smooth. Stir in the muesli.

Step three Spoon 28 teaspoonfuls of the mixture onto the prepared baking trays, leaving room for the cookies to spread. Sprinkle the top of each one with a little extra muesli and a little demerara sugar.

Step four Bake in the preheated oven for 10–15 minutes or until golden brown at the edges. Lift onto a wire rack to cool.

Almond Tuiles

These slim, crisp, curled biscuits are wonderful with light mousses, ice cream and fruit salads. They keep well in an airtight tin or, if made a long time in advance, in the freezer. Store them in a rigid box or tin so they cannot be broken.

Step one Preheat the oven to 200°C/fan 180°C/gas 6. Lightly butter the baking trays.

Step two Measure the butter and sugar into a bowl and beat well together until pale and fluffy. Sift the flour over the egg white, mix and then stir into the butter mixture along with the finely chopped almonds. Place teaspoonfuls of the mixture, about four at a time, onto the prepared baking trays leaving ample room for the biscuits to spread.

Step three Bake the first four biscuits in the preheated oven for 6–8 minutes or until they are browned around the edge but not in the middle. Remove from the oven and place the next batch of four biscuits in to bake.

Step four Leave the first batch to stand for a second or two, then remove from the trays with a palette knife and curl over a rolling pin until set. Place four more teaspoons of the mixture on the tray ready to go into the oven when the second batch comes out. Carry on baking and curling the biscuits in this way until you have finished all 20 biscuits. When cool, store in an airtight container. Serve with a dusting of icing sugar, if liked.

Makes 20

Equipment needed:
2 baking trays

75g (3oz) butter, softened

75g (3oz) caster sugar

50g (2oz) plain flour

1 large egg white

75g (3oz) finely chopped blanched almonds

to finish

icing sugar, for dusting, optional

Macaroons

Traditionally, macaroons were always made on rice paper but, as this is not always easy to get hold of, I've used non-stick baking parchment.

Makes 16

Equipment needed:
2 baking trays

2 large egg whites

8 blanched
almonds, halved

100g (4oz)
ground almonds

175g (6oz)
caster sugar

25g (1oz) ground
rice or semolina

few drops
almond extract

Step one Preheat the oven to 150°C/fan 130°C/gas 2. Line the baking trays with non-stick baking parchment.

Step two Put the egg whites into a bowl, dip in the halved almonds and set them aside. Whisk the egg whites until they form soft peaks. Gently fold in the ground almonds, sugar, ground rice or semolina and almond extract.

Step three Spoon the mixture in teaspoonfuls onto the prepared baking trays, and smooth out with the back of a spoon to form circles. Place an almond half in the centre of each.

Step four Bake in the preheated oven for 20–25 minutes or until a pale golden brown. Leave to cool on the trays for a few minutes, then lift off and finish cooling on a wire rack.

Sugared Pretzels

I use a quick method for making the pastry here rather than the classic way.

Step one Measure the flour into a large bowl, add the butter and rub in with your fingertips until the mixture resembles fine breadcrumbs. Stir in the sugar and then the egg and vanilla extract and mix until the pastry comes together. Knead very gently on a lightly floured work surface until smooth, then wrap in clingfilm and chill for about 30 minutes, or until firm enough to roll.

Step two Preheat the oven to 200°C/fan 180°C/gas 6. Lightly butter the baking trays.

Step three Divide the dough into 16 pieces about the size of a walnut. Roll each piece into a thin sausage shape and then twist into the traditional pretzel shape, like a loose knot. Place on the prepared baking trays.

Step four Bake in the preheated oven for about 8 minutes or until barely changing colour. Lift onto a wire rack and dust thickly with icing sugar while still hot.

Makes 16

Equipment needed:
2 baking trays

115g (4½ oz)
plain flour

65g (2½ oz) butter

25g (1oz) caster sugar

1 large egg, beaten

few drops vanilla
extract

to finish

icing sugar,
for dusting

Easter Biscuits

The Easter Biscuits you buy are usually larger than this. If you like them that way, simply use a larger cutter.

Makes 24

Equipment needed:
3 baking trays

100g (4oz) butter, softened

75g (3oz) caster sugar

1 large egg, separated

200g (7oz) plain flour

½ level tsp mixed spice

½ level tsp ground cinnamon

50g (2oz) currants

25g (1oz) chopped candied peel

1–2 tbsp milk

caster sugar, for sprinkling

Step one Preheat the oven to 200°C/fan 180°C/gas 6. Lightly butter the baking trays.

Step two Measure the butter and sugar into a bowl and beat together until light and fluffy. Beat in the egg yolk. Sift in the flour and spices and mix well. Add the currants and chopped candied peel and enough milk to give a fairly soft dough.

Step three Knead the mixture gently on a lightly floured work surface and roll out to a thickness of 5mm (¼in). Cut into rounds using a 6cm (2½in) fluted cutter. Place on the prepared baking trays.

Step four Bake in the preheated oven for 8–10 minutes. Meanwhile, lightly beat the egg white. Remove the biscuits from the oven, brush them with the beaten egg white, sprinkle with a little caster sugar and return to the oven for a further 4–5 minutes or until pale golden brown. Lift onto a wire rack to cool. Store in an airtight container.

If homemade or bought biscuits have gone a little soft, place them on a baking tray and crisp them in a moderate oven for a few minutes.

Brandy Snaps

These delicious treats can be served plain with ice cream or mousses, or filled with whipped cream and served with fruit.

Step one Preheat the oven to 160°C/fan 140°C/gas 3. Line the baking trays with non-stick baking parchment and then oil the handles of four wooden spoons.

Step two Measure the butter, sugar and syrup into a small pan and heat gently until the butter has melted and the sugar has dissolved. Leave the mixture to cool slightly and then sift in the flour and the ginger. Add the lemon juice and stir well to mix thoroughly. Place teaspoonfuls of the mixture, at least 10cm (4in) apart, onto the prepared baking trays, putting only four on each tray. Place one tray in the oven and set the second aside.

Step three Bake the four biscuits in the preheated oven for about 8 minutes or until the mixture is well spread out and a dark golden colour. Remove from the oven and leave for a few minutes to become firm, then lift them from the baking parchment using a fish slice. Turn over and roll around the handle of the wooden spoons. Leave to set on a wire rack and then slide out the spoons. Place the second set of four biscuits into the oven. Repeat the entire process, baking four biscuits at a time, until all the Brandy Snaps have been formed.

Step four When cold, store them in an airtight tin. If you would like to serve them filled with cream, use a piping bag fitted with a plain nozzle to fill them with a little of the whipped cream. These can be covered and stored in the refrigerator for up to 2 hours before serving.

Makes 24

Equipment needed:
2 baking trays

vegetable oil, for oiling the wooden spoon handles

50g (2oz) butter

50g (2oz) demerara sugar

50g (2oz) golden syrup

50g (2oz) plain flour

½ level tsp ground ginger

½ tsp lemon juice

300ml (½ pint) whipping or double cream (not extra thick), whipped, (optional)

Anzac Biscuits

Also known as Diggers, these traditional Australian biscuits are really easy to make.

Makes 45

Equipment needed:
2 baking trays

150g (5oz) butter, softened

1 tbsp golden syrup

175g (6oz) sugar

75g (3oz)
self-raising flour

75g (3oz)
desiccated coconut

100g (4oz)
porridge oats

Step one Preheat the oven to 180°C/fan 160°C/gas 4. Lightly butter the baking trays.

Step two Measure the butter, golden syrup and sugar into a medium pan and heat gently until the butter has melted and the sugar has dissolved. Stir in the flour, coconut and oats and mix well until evenly blended.

Step three Place large teaspoonfuls of the mixture spaced well apart on the prepared baking trays and flatten slightly with the back of the spoon. You should have enough mixture for about 45 mounds, and you will need to bake them in batches.

Step four Bake in the preheated oven for 8–10 minutes or until they have spread out flat and are lightly browned at the edges. Leave to cool on the trays for a few minutes, then carefully lift off with a palette knife and place on a wire rack to cool completely. If the biscuits harden too much to lift off the tray, pop them back in the oven for a few minutes to soften. Store in an airtight container.

Gingerbread Men

Children love to cut out and decorate these biscuits. I use a 13.5cm (5½in) gingerbread man cutter to make 20 gingerbread men from this mixture.

Step one Preheat the oven to 190°C/fan 170°C/gas 5. Lightly butter the baking trays.

Step two Measure the flour, bicarbonate of soda and ginger into a bowl. Rub in the butter with your fingertips until the mixture resembles fine breadcrumbs, then stir in the sugar. Add the golden syrup and beaten egg and mix to form a smooth dough, kneading lightly with your hands towards the end.

Step three Divide the dough in half and roll out one half to a thickness of about 5mm (¼in) on a lightly floured work surface. Cut out 10 gingerbread men using a gingerbread man cutter, and place them onto the prepared baking trays. Use the currants for eyes and buttons. Repeat with the remaining dough.

Step four Bake in the preheated oven for about 10–12 minutes or until they become a slightly darker shade. Cool slightly, then lift onto a wire rack and leave to cool completely.

Makes 20

Equipment needed:
3 baking trays

350g (12oz) plain flour

1 level tsp
bicarbonate of soda

2 tsp ground ginger

100g (4oz) butter

175g (6oz) light
muscovado sugar

4 tbsp golden syrup

1 large egg, beaten

currants, to decorate

Iced Animal Biscuits

Let the children ice the animals themselves with their favourite colours. Animal cutters are available from good cook shops.

Makes 50

Equipment needed:
2 baking trays

225g (8oz)
self-raising flour

100g (4oz) butter,
softened

few drops
vanilla extract

100g (4oz)
caster sugar

1 large egg, beaten

1 tbsp milk

for the icing

100g (4oz) icing sugar

1 tbsp lemon juice

food colouring (red,
green, brown, pink or
yellow)

Step one Preheat the oven to 190°C/fan 170°C/gas 5. Lightly butter the baking trays.

Step two Measure the flour into a mixing bowl and rub in the butter with your fingertips until the mixture resembles fine breadcrumbs. Add the vanilla extract, sugar, beaten egg and milk and mix to form a fairly stiff dough. Roll out thinly on a lightly floured work surface, and cut into 50 animal shapes using cutters. Place on the prepared baking trays.

Step three Bake in the preheated oven for 10–15 minutes or until golden brown. Cool on a wire rack.

Step four To make the icing, sift the icing sugar into a bowl and add enough lemon juice to give a spreading consistency. Divide the icing between 2–3 small bowls (cups would do) and add a drop of different food colouring to each bowl, mixing well. Spoon a little icing onto each of the biscuits and spread out with the back of a teaspoon. Finish by adding dots of contrasting food colouring for the eyes and other details.

Food colouring pens are useful for adding details like wings, feet and facial features. If you like, you can use tiny edible metallic balls in a wide range of colours, including gold and silver, for the eyes.

Jumbles

It is usual to shape this mixture into 'S' shapes, but of course you can shape it into any letter or number of your choice.

Step one Lightly butter the baking trays. Measure all the ingredients except the honey and demerara sugar into a bowl and work together by hand until a dough is formed. This can also be done in a food processor or with an electric mixer.

Step two Divide the dough into 32 pieces. Roll each piece of dough into a strip about 10cm (4in) long, then twist them into 'S' shapes. Put them on the baking trays and chill for about 30 minutes. Preheat the oven to 190°C/fan 170°C/gas 5.

Step three Bake the jumbles in the preheated oven for 10–15 minutes or until they are a pale golden colour, then remove from the oven. Turn the oven up to 220°C/fan 200°C/gas 7 and, while the jumbles are still warm, brush them well with honey and sprinkle with demerara sugar. Return to the oven for 2–3 minutes or until the sugar has caramelised. Cool on a wire rack.

Makes 32

Equipment needed:
3 baking trays

150g (5oz) butter, softened

150g (5oz) caster sugar

a few drops vanilla extract

finely grated zest of 1 lemon

1 large egg

350g (12oz) plain flour

clear honey, for glazing

demerara sugar, for dusting

Iced Lemon Traybake

You can vary a basic traybake quite simply – in this case by adding
a subtle lemon flavour and a lemon glacé icing.

Makes 21 pieces

Cake tin needed:
a 30 x 23cm
(12 x 9in) traybake
or roasting tin

225g (8oz) butter,
softened

225g (8oz)
caster sugar

275g (10oz)
self-raising flour

2 level tsp
baking powder

4 large eggs

4 tbsp milk

grated zest
of 2 lemons

for the glacé icing

3 tbsp lemon juice

225g (8oz) sifted
icing sugar

Step one Preheat the oven to 180°C/fan 160°C/gas 4. Butter
the tin, then line the base with non-stick baking parchment.

Step two Measure all the cake ingredients into a large bowl
and beat until well blended. Turn the mixture into the prepared
tin and level the top.

Step three Bake in the preheated oven for 35–40 minutes or
until the cake has shrunk from the sides of the tin and springs
back when pressed in the centre with your fingertips. Leave to
cool in the tin.

Step four Mix together the lemon juice and icing sugar to give
a runny consistency. Spread out evenly over the cake and leave
to set before cutting into 21 pieces.

Chocolate Chip Brownies

A really simple brownie recipe – just measure all the ingredients into a bowl and give it a good mix! Be careful not to overcook your brownies: they should have a slightly gooey texture. The outside crust should be on the crisp side, though, thanks to the high proportion of sugar.

Step one Preheat the oven to 180°C/fan 160°C/gas 4. Butter the tin, then line the base and sides with non-stick baking parchment.

Step two Measure all the ingredients into a large bowl and beat until evenly blended. Spoon the mixture into the prepared tin, scraping the sides of the bowl with a plastic spatula to remove all of it. Spread the mixture gently to the corners of the tin and level the top with the back of the spatula.

Step three Bake in the preheated oven for 40–45 minutes or until the brownies have a crusty top and a skewer inserted into the centre comes out clean. Cover loosely with foil for the last 10 minutes if the mixture is browning too much. Leave the brownies to cool in the tin and then cut into 24 squares. Store in an airtight tin.

Makes 24 squares

Cake tin needed:
a 30 x 23cm
(12 x 9in) traybake
or roasting tin

275g (10oz) butter, softened

375g (13oz) caster sugar

4 large eggs

75g (3oz) cocoa powder

100g (4oz) self-raising flour

100g (4oz) plain chocolate chips

For Mary Berry's baking tips, go to
www.mykitchentable.co.uk/authors/MaryBerry/bakingtips

Millionaires' Shortbread

This shortbread is always popular. The different textures are the principal appeal – the crunch of the shortbread base, the caramel in the middle, and the chunky chocolate on top.

Makes 24 bars

Cake tin needed:
a 33 x 23cm (13 x 9in)
Swiss roll tin

for the shortbread

250g (9oz) plain flour

75g (3oz)
caster sugar

175g (6oz) butter,
softened

for the caramel

100g (4oz) butter

100g (4oz) light
muscovado sugar

2 x 397g (14oz) tins
full-fat condensed milk

for the topping

200g (7oz) plain
chocolate (39 per cent
cocoa solids) or milk
chocolate

Step one Preheat the oven to 180°C/fan 160°C/gas 4. Lightly butter the tin.

Step two Measure the flour and caster sugar into a bowl. Rub in the butter until the mixture resembles fine breadcrumbs.

Step three Knead the mixture together until it forms a dough, then press into the base of the prepared tin. Prick the shortbread lightly with a fork and bake in the preheated oven for about 20 minutes or until firm to the touch and very lightly browned. Cool in the tin.

Step four Meanwhile, to make the caramel, measure the butter, sugar and condensed milk into a pan and heat gently until the sugar has dissolved. Bring to the boil, stirring all the time, then reduce the heat and simmer very gently, for about 5 minutes or until the mixture has thickened slightly. Stir continuously – if you leave it for even a second, it will catch on the bottom and burn. Pour over the shortbread and leave to cool.

Step five To make the topping, break the chocolate into pieces into a heatproof bowl and place over a pan of barely simmering water or in a microwave, taking care not to burn the chocolate, and stirring occasionally. Pour over the cold caramel and leave to set. Cut into squares or bars.

A marbled chocolate top looks stunning. Melt just over 50g (2oz) each of plain (39 per cent cocoa solids), milk and white chocolate in separate bowls. Place the chocolate in spoonfuls over the set caramel, alternating the three. Use a skewer to marble the edges of the chocolates together and leave to set.

American Spiced Carrot Traybake

Bought mixtures of chopped nuts might include a high proportion of peanuts. I always prefer to make up my own mix from shelled nuts.

Step one Preheat the oven to 180°C/fan 160°C/gas 4. Butter the tin, then line the base with non-stick baking parchment.

Step two Measure all the dry cake ingredients into a large bowl. Add the oil, grated carrots, eggs (one at a time) and vanilla extract, beating between each addition. Pour into the prepared tin and level the surface.

Step three Bake in the preheated oven for 50–60 minutes or until the cake is well risen, golden brown in colour and firm to the touch. Leave to cool in the tin for 10 minutes, then turn out, peel off the parchment and finish cooling on a wire rack.

Step four To make the topping, mix together the cheese, honey and lemon juice, adding, if necessary, a little extra lemon juice to make a spreading consistency. Spread evenly over the cake with a palette knife, then sprinkle over the very finely chopped nuts to decorate and cut into 16 pieces. You can store the iced cake in the fridge for up to 2 weeks.

Makes 16 pieces

Cake tin needed:
a 30 x 23cm
(12 x 9in) traybake
or roasting tin

275g (10oz)
self-raising flour

350g (12oz)
caster sugar

2 level tsp
baking powder

75g (3oz) chopped
unsalted mixed nuts

3 level tsp
ground cinnamon

2 level tsp
ground ginger

300ml (½ pint)
sunflower oil

275g (10oz)
grated carrots

4 large eggs

1 tsp vanilla extract

for the topping

400g (14oz) full-fat
soft cheese

4 tsp clear honey

2 tsp lemon juice

very finely chopped
mixed unsalted nuts,
to decorate

Orange Drop Scones

Serve as soon as they are made, with butter and syrup. If you want to make them in advance and need to reheat them, arrange them in a single layer on an ovenproof plate, cover tightly with foil and reheat in a moderate oven for about 10 minutes.

Makes 24

Cookware needed:
a large non-stick
frying pan

2 oranges

a little milk

175g (6oz)
self-raising flour

1 level tsp
baking powder

40g (1½ oz)
caster sugar

1 large egg

vegetable oil or white
vegetable fat, for
frying

Step one Grate the zest from the oranges and set aside, and then squeeze the juice. Pour the juice into a measuring jug and make it up to 200ml (7fl oz) with milk.

Step two Measure the flour, baking powder, sugar and orange zest into a mixing bowl. Make a well in the centre and add the egg and half the orange juice and milk mixture. Beat well to make a smooth, thick batter and then beat in enough of the remaining orange juice and milk to give a batter the consistency of thick cream.

Step three Heat the frying pan over a medium heat and grease with a little oil or white vegetable fat. Drop the mixture in dessertspoonfuls into the hot pan, spacing them well apart to allow the mixture to spread.

Step four When bubbles appear on the surface, turn the scones over with a palette knife and cook on the other side for 30 seconds–1 minute or until golden brown. Transfer to a wire rack and cover with a clean tea towel.

Step five Cook the remaining mixture in the same way. Serve warm, with butter and golden or maple syrup and a little extra grated orange zest, if liked.

Treacle Spice Traybake

This is one for those who like the rich flavour of treacle in baking. Don't be too worried if the traybake dips in the centre – it just means you were a little generous with the treacle.

Step one Preheat the oven to 180°C/fan 160°C/gas 4. Butter the tin, then line the base with non-stick baking parchment.

Step two Measure all the ingredients into a large bowl and beat well for about 2 minutes or until well blended. Turn the mixture into the prepared tin and level the top.

Step three Bake in the preheated oven for 35–40 minutes or until the cake has shrunk from the sides of the tin and springs back when pressed in the centre with your fingertips. Leave to cool in the tin, then cut into 21 pieces.

These spicy squares can be dusted with sifted icing sugar to serve, if you like.

Makes 21 pieces

Cake tin needed:
a 30 x 23cm
(12 x 9in) traybake
or roasting tin

225g (8oz) butter,
softened

175g (6oz)
caster sugar

225g (8oz)
black treacle

275g (10oz)
self-raising flour

2 level tsp
baking powder

2 level tsp ground
mixed spice

4 large eggs, beaten

4 tbsp milk

Date and Cherry Butter Bars

It's important to use butter and not baking margarine in this recipe, to achieve a lovely buttery flavour.

Makes 24

Cake tin needed:
a 30 x 23cm
(12 x 9in) traybake
or roasting tin

225g (8oz)
self-raising flour

½ level tsp
baking powder

75g (3oz) butter

100g (4oz)
caster sugar

75g (3oz)
chopped dates

25g (1oz) chopped
red or natural
glacé cherries

1 large egg, beaten

Step one Preheat the oven to 190°C/fan 170°C/gas 5. Butter the tin.

Step two Measure the flour and baking powder into a bowl and rub in the butter using your fingertips until the mixture resembles fine breadcrumbs. Stir in the sugar, chopped dates and chopped cherries. Add the beaten egg and bring the mixture together to form a dough. Knead lightly until smooth, then press into the prepared tin.

Step three Bake in the preheated oven for about 10 minutes then remove from the oven and cut into 24 bars. Return to the oven for about 10 minutes or until starting to tinge a golden colour. Re-cut into bars and leave to cool in the tin. When cold, ease the bars out and store in an airtight container.

Date and Walnut Traybake

This is a deliciously nutty and rich traybake. The addition of chopped dates makes it enticingly moist.

Step one Preheat the oven to 180°C/fan 160°C/gas 4. Butter the tin, then line the base with non-stick baking parchment.

Step two Measure the dates and butter into a small bowl and pour over the boiling water. Set aside to cool. Meanwhile, whisk the eggs and sugar together in a large bowl. Then add the cooled date mixture and the remaining cake ingredients. Whisk, then pour into the prepared tin.

Step three Bake in the preheated oven for about 1 hour 10 minutes or until the cake is firm to the touch and golden brown in colour. Leave to cool in the tin for 10 minutes, then turn out, peel off the parchment and finish cooling on a wire rack.

Step four To make the icing, mix the icing sugar with the lemon zest and juice, adding a little hot water to make a spreading consistency. Pour over the cake and gently spread out evenly with a palette knife. Decorate with walnut pieces and leave to set, then cut into 21 pieces.

Makes 21 pieces

Cake tin needed:
a 30 x 23cm
(12 x 9in) traybake
or roasting tin

250g (9oz) stoned
and chopped dates

40g (1½ oz) butter,
softened

350ml (12fl oz)
boiling water

2 large eggs

200g (7oz) dark
muscovado sugar

150g (5oz)
ground almonds

150g (5oz)
chopped walnuts

350g (12oz)
self-raising flour

1½ level tsp
ground cinnamon

for the icing

225g (8oz) sifted
icing sugar

grated zest and
juice of 1 lemon

walnut pieces,
to decorate

Apricot and Walnut Sandwich Bars

These luscious, moist bars are similar to those you can buy in health-food shops, and are quite substantial and wholesome additions to a lunch box.

Makes 8

Cake tin needed:
an 18cm (7in) shallow
square cake tin

for the filling

175g (6oz)
ready-to-eat
dried apricots

2 tbsp caster sugar

grated zest of 1 lemon

for the oat mixture

50g (2oz)
porridge oats

50g (2oz) light
muscovado sugar

40g (1½ oz)
chopped walnuts

200g (7oz) wholemeal
self-raising flour

175g (6oz)
butter, melted

Step one Preheat the oven to 150°C/fan 130°C/gas 2. Butter the tin, then line the base with non-stick baking parchment.

Step two First, prepare the filling. Snip the apricots into pieces and put them in a small pan with 50ml (2fl oz) water, caster sugar and lemon zest. Bring to the boil and then simmer very gently until the apricots are really soft and the liquid has evaporated. Set aside to cool.

Step three While the apricot filling is cooling, make the oat mixture. Measure the oats, sugar, walnuts and flour into a bowl and add the melted butter. Stir to mix. Divide the oat mixture in half and spread one half over the base of the prepared tin. Spoon the cooled apricot mixture on top and carefully spread it to form an even layer. Cover evenly with the remaining oat mixture.

Step four Bake in the preheated oven for about 45 minutes or until firm and golden brown. Cut into bars while still warm.

Coconut Pyramids

You can use a dariole mould or an eggcup for these easy-to-make little cakes, or you could buy a pyramid mould for a more pointed shape.

Step one Preheat the oven to 180°C/fan 160°C/gas 4. Line the baking trays with non-stick baking parchment.

Step two Measure the coconut and sugar into a bowl and mix together. Beat in enough egg to bind the mixture together.

Step three Dip the mould or eggcup into cold water and drain it well. Fill with the coconut mixture and press down lightly. Turn the moulded coconut out onto a baking tray and continue with the remaining mixture.

Step four Bake in the preheated oven for about 20 minutes or until the pyramids are tinged pale golden brown. Lift off the baking trays and arrange on a wire rack. Place a halved glacé cherry on top of each and leave to cool.

Makes 12

Equipment needed:
2 baking trays

a dariole mould or an eggcup

225g (8oz) desiccated coconut

100g (4oz) caster sugar

2 large eggs, beaten

6 glacé cherries, halved, to decorate

Iced Chocolate Traybake with Fudge Icing

Chocolate cakes are always popular, and this is a particularly simple version. We often serve it as a dessert by pouring the hot icing over the top.

Makes 21 pieces

Cake tin needed:
a 30 x 23cm
(12 x 9in) traybake
or roasting tin

4 level tbsp
cocoa powder

225g (8oz) butter,
softened

225g (8oz)
caster sugar

275g (10oz)
self-raising flour

2 level tsp
baking powder

4 large eggs

4 tbsp milk

for the icing and decoration

4 level tbsp
apricot jam

50g (2oz) butter

25g (1oz) cocoa
powder, sifted

3 tbsp milk

225g (8oz) icing
sugar, sifted

chocolate, for making
curls, to decorate

Step one Preheat the oven to 180°C/fan 160°C/gas 4. Butter the tin, then line the base with non-stick baking parchment.

Step two Blend together the cocoa powder and 4 tablespoons hot water, then allow to cool slightly. Measure all the cake ingredients into a large bowl, add the cocoa mixture and beat until well blended. Turn the mixture into the prepared tin and level the surface.

Step three Bake for 35–40 minutes or until the cake has shrunk from the sides of the tin and the centre of the cake springs back when pressed with your fingertips. Leave to cool in the tin.

Step four Warm the apricot jam in a pan and brush all over the cake. Then melt the butter in a small pan, add the cocoa powder, stir to blend and cook gently for 1 minute. Stir in the milk and icing sugar, remove from the heat and mix very well, then leave on one side, stirring occasionally, until the icing thickens.

Step five Pour over the cold cake and smooth over gently with a palette knife. Leave to set for about 30 minutes, then cut into pieces. To make the chocolate curls, let the chocolate come to room temperature and then shave using a vegetable peeler. Decorate the pieces with the chocolate curls and serve.

Marmalade Traybake

Be careful when measuring the marmalade. If you put too much in, the traybake will dip in the centre.

Step one Preheat the oven to 180°C/fan 160°C/gas 4. Butter the tin, then line the base with non-stick baking parchment.

Step two Measure all the ingredients, except the nibbed sugar, into a large bowl and beat until thoroughly blended. Turn into the prepared tin and smooth the top, then sprinkle with the nibbed sugar.

Step three Bake in the preheated oven for 40–45 minutes or until well risen, golden brown and firm to the touch. Leave to cool in the tin for 10 minutes, then turn out, peel off the parchment and finish cooling on a wire rack. When cool, cut into 24 pieces.

Instead of nibbed sugar, you could use crushed sugar cubes.

Makes 24 pieces

Cake tin needed:
a 30 x 23cm
(12 x 9in) traybake
or roasting tin

175g (6oz) butter,
softened

175g (6oz)
caster sugar

175g (6oz) sultanas

175g (6oz) currants

3 large eggs, beaten

250g (9oz)
self-raising flour

1½ level tsp
baking powder

50g (2oz) quartered
red or natural
glacé cherries

2 level tbsp
marmalade

3 tbsp milk

nibbed sugar,
to decorate

Coffee and Cinnamon American Muffins

These large muffins look quite impressive. They're best eaten on the day of baking.

Makes 12

Equipment needed:
a 12-hole muffin tin

250g (9oz)
self-raising flour

1 level tsp
baking powder

1 heaped tsp ground
cinnamon

50g (2oz) butter,
softened

2 tsp instant coffee
granules

75g (3oz) caster sugar

2 large eggs

250ml (9fl oz) milk

Step one Preheat the oven to 200°C/fan 180°C/gas 6. Place muffin cases into the muffin tin.

Step two Measure the flour, baking powder and cinnamon into a mixing bowl. Add the butter and rub into the flour with your fingertips until the mixture resembles fine breadcrumbs. Measure the coffee into a mug and add 1 tablespoon boiling water. Mix to a smooth paste. Stir the coffee mixture and the sugar into the flour mixture.

Step three Mix together the eggs and milk, then pour into the dry ingredients. Mix with a wooden spoon to blend to a lumpy consistency. Spoon the mixture into the muffin cases, filling them almost to the top.

Step four Bake for 20–25 minutes or until well risen and firm to the touch. Leave to cool for a few minutes in the tin, then lift out the paper cases and cool the muffins for a little longer on a wire rack.

Chocolate Cupcakes with Ganache Icing

Cupcakes are great for teatime, or arranged stacked on a cake stand instead of a large traditional birthday cake or even a wedding cake. Cupcakes are a different shape from fairy cakes – the cases they are baked in are deeper and have less angular sides.

Step one Preheat the oven to 180°C/fan 160°C/gas 4. Put the muffin cases into the muffin tin, so that the cakes keep a good even shape as they bake.

Step two Measure the cocoa into a large bowl. Heat the milk until hot and pour it over the cocoa. Stir until you have a smooth paste. Add the remaining cupcake ingredients and beat until blended and smooth. Spoon evenly between the paper cases.

Step three Bake for 20–25 minutes or until risen and golden brown. Lift the paper cases out of the tin and cool the cakes on a wire rack until completely cold before icing.

Step four To make the ganache icing, heat the cream in a pan and, when scalding, drop the chocolate cubes into the hot cream. Stir until smooth and shiny. Set aside to cool and thicken until it is the perfect spreading or piping consistency. Spread or pipe the icing over the cupcakes and decorate with plain or white chocolate curls or shavings.

If you are making a double quantity of cupcakes or are using a smaller tin, you can prepare your cupcake mixture in one go and spoon it into the paper cases ready to go into the oven. They will come to no harm, as raising agents react more slowly nowadays. Bake only one tray of cupcakes at a time, though.

Makes 12

Equipment needed: a 12-hole muffin tin

25g (1oz) cocoa powder

3 tbsp milk

100g (4oz) butter, softened

100g (4oz) self-raising flour

150g (5oz) caster sugar

2 large eggs

for the ganache icing

50ml (2fl oz) double cream (not extra thick)

60g (2½ oz) plain chocolate (39 per cent cocoa solids), chopped into cubes

to decorate

plain or white chocolate curls (see page 80) or shavings

Spiced Cherry Rock Cakes

These are very traditional English cakes, but this version is slightly different, with the addition of cherries and spice. They're inexpensive, can be large or tiny, and need no special equipment. They are best eaten on the day of making.

Makes 12

Equipment needed:
2 baking trays

225g (8oz)
self-raising flour

2 level tsp
baking powder

100g (4oz) butter,
softened

50g (2oz) sugar

150g (5oz) glacé
cherries, rinsed,
dried and quartered

1 level tsp ground
mixed spice

1 large egg

about 1 tbsp milk

a little demerara
sugar, for sprinkling

Step one Preheat the oven to 200°C/fan 180°C/gas 6. Lightly butter the baking trays.

Step two Measure the flour and baking powder into a large bowl, add the butter and rub in with your fingertips until the mixture resembles fine breadcrumbs. Stir in the sugar, cherries and spice.

Step three Beat the egg and milk together and add to the fruity mixture. If the mixture is too dry, add a little more milk. Using a pair of teaspoons, shape the mixture into about 12 rough mounds and place on the prepared baking trays. Sprinkle generously with demerara sugar.

Step four Bake in the preheated oven for about 15 minutes or until a pale golden brown at the edges. Cool on a wire rack.

Use wholemeal self-raising flour, if you like, although you may need to add a little more milk to the mix.

Banana and Chocolate Chip Bars

These bars make a really healthy snack. The banana in the middle could be replaced with ready-to-eat dried apricots.

Step one Preheat the oven to 180°C/fan 160°C/gas 4. Lightly butter the tin.

Step two Mix together the flour, oats and sugar in a large bowl. Rub in the butter with your fingertips until the mixture resembles breadcrumbs. Spread half the mixture over the base of the tin and arrange the sliced banana on top. Sprinkle over the remaining crumb mixture and press down well. Top with the chocolate chips.

Step three Bake in the preheated oven for about 25 minutes or until golden brown. Leave in the tin until cold and then cut into bars to serve.

Makes 12

Cake tin needed: an 18cm (7in) square shallow cake tin

75g (3oz) wholemeal self-raising flour

75g (3oz) porridge oats

75g (3oz) demerara sugar

100g (4oz) butter, softened

1 ripe banana, sliced

25g (1oz) chocolate chips

Double Ginger Muffins

These are best served warm. Don't expect them to be sweet, like a cake, because they are more like scones. Crystallised stem ginger comes in a jar in ginger syrup. It is not traditional to ice a muffin but, if you like, sift some icing sugar into some of the ginger syrup to make a tasty icing.

Makes 12

Equipment needed:
a 12-hole muffin tin

275g (10oz) plain flour

1 level tsp
baking powder

75g (3oz) caster sugar

½ level tsp ground
ginger

2 large eggs

225ml (8fl oz) milk

100g (4oz) butter,
melted and cooled

4 bulbs crystallised
stem ginger, cut into
tiny raisin-sized pieces

Step one Preheat the oven to 200°C/fan 180°C/gas 6. Butter the muffin tin, or put a paper muffin case into each muffin hole, or place the muffin cases directly onto a baking sheet.

Step two Measure the flour, baking powder, sugar and ground ginger into a mixing bowl and stir briefly to combine.

Step three Mix together the eggs, milk and cooled melted butter and then add these to the dry ingredients. Mix quickly but gently to blend the ingredients together. Don't overmix; it doesn't need to be a smooth mixture, as long as the dry ingredients are incorporated. Stir in the ginger pieces.

Step four Spoon the mixture into the muffin tin holes or individual cases, filling each hole or case almost to the top. Bake for 20–25 minutes or until well risen, golden and firm to the touch. Allow to cool for a few minutes in the tin, then lift out and cool for a little longer on a wire rack. Serve warm.

If you have made the muffins ahead and want to reheat them, pop them in a low oven for a few minutes.

Gingerbread Traybake

This gingerbread is equally delicious without the icing, and is perfect for a packed lunch.

Step one Preheat the oven to 160°C/fan 140°C/gas 3. Butter the tin, then line the base with non-stick baking parchment.

Step two Measure the syrup, treacle, sugar and butter into a large pan and heat gently until the butter has melted. Remove from the heat and stir in the flour and spices. Add the beaten eggs and milk, and beat until smooth. Pour into the prepared tin.

Step three Bake in the preheated oven for 45–50 minutes or until the cake has shrunk from the sides of the tin and springs back when pressed in the centre with your fingertips. Leave to cool in the tin for a few minutes, then turn out, peel off the parchment and finish cooling on a wire rack.

Step four To make the icing, sift the icing sugar into a bowl, add 2 tablespoons water a little at a time, and mix until smooth. Spoon over the cake, then scatter over the chopped ginger. Leave to set, then cut into 21 pieces.

Heat the syrup and other ingredients through very gently. If they are too hot when the flour is stirred in, the mixture could go lumpy. If it does, you'll have to rub it through a sieve.

Makes 21 pieces

Cake tin needed:
a 30 x 23cm
(12 x 9in) traybake
or roasting tin

275g (10oz)
golden syrup

275g (10oz)
black treacle

225g (8oz) light
muscovado sugar

225g (8oz) butter,
softened

450g (1lb)
self-raising flour

2 level tsp ground
mixed spice

2 level tsp
ground ginger

4 large eggs,
lightly beaten

4 tbsp milk

for the icing

225g (8oz) icing sugar

50g (2oz) finely
chopped crystallised
or stem ginger, to
decorate

Wholemeal Sultana and Apricot Rock Cakes

Wholemeal flours can vary in the amount of liquid they absorb, so be ready to add a little more milk, if necessary. Wholemeal rock cakes tend to be drier than normal ones, and they are best eaten on the day of baking.

Makes 12

Equipment needed:
2 baking trays

100g (4oz)
self-raising flour

100g (4oz) wholemeal
self-raising flour

2 level tsp
baking powder

100g (4oz) butter,
softened

50g (2oz) light
muscovado sugar

50g (2oz) sultanas

50g (2oz) chopped
ready-to-eat dried
apricots

1 large egg

about 2 tbsp milk

a little demerara
sugar, for sprinkling

Step one Preheat the oven to 200°C/fan 180°C/gas 6. Lightly butter the baking trays.

Step two Measure the flours and baking powder into a large bowl, add the butter and rub into the flour with your fingertips until the mixture resembles fine breadcrumbs. Stir in the sugar, sultanas and chopped apricots.

Step three Beat the egg and milk together and add to the fruity mixture. If it is too dry, add a little more milk. Using a pair of teaspoons, shape the mixture into about 12 rough mounds on the prepared baking trays and sprinkle each mound generously with demerara sugar.

Step four Bake in the preheated oven for about 15 minutes or until beginning to tinge with brown at the edges. Cool on a wire rack.

Bakewell Slices

Be generous with the raspberry jam – it makes all the difference.
As the shortcrust pastry contains a lot of fat and no sugar, there is
no need to line the tin with non-stick baking parchment.

Step one To make the pastry, measure the flour into a bowl
and rub in the butter with your fingertips until the mixture
resembles fine breadcrumbs. Add 2–3 tablespoons cold water
gradually, mixing to form a soft dough.

Step two Preheat the oven to 180°C/fan 160°C/gas 4. Roll the
dough out on a lightly floured work surface and use it to line
the tin.

Step three Measure all the sponge ingredients into a bowl and
beat until well blended. Spread the pastry with raspberry jam
and then top with the sponge mixture. Sprinkle with the flaked
almonds.

Step four Bake in the preheated oven for about 25 minutes or
until the cake has shrunk from the sides of the tin and springs
back when pressed in the centre with your fingertips. Leave to
cool in the tin and then cut into slices.

Makes 24

Cake tin needed:
a 30 x 23cm
(12 x 9in) traybake
or roasting tin

**for the shortcrust
pastry**

175g (6oz) plain flour

75g (3oz) butter

for the sponge mixture

100g (4oz) butter,
softened

100g (4oz)
caster sugar

175g (6oz)
self-raising flour

1 level tsp
baking powder

2 large eggs

2 tbsp milk

⅛ tsp almond extract

to finish

about 4 tbsp
raspberry jam

flaked almonds,
for sprinkling

Toffee Marshmallow Squares

Although these squares are not baked in the oven I have included this recipe here because it is very popular with all children. And, with supervision, even very young ones can make them.

Makes 20 squares

Cake tin needed:
a 30 x 23cm (12 x 9in)
oblong baking tin

100g (4oz) butter

100g (4oz)
marshmallows

100g (4oz)
dairy toffees

150g (5oz) small
puffed-rice cereal

Step one Measure the butter, marshmallows and toffees into a thick-based pan and heat gently until the mixture is melted and smooth. This will take about 5 minutes.

Step two Place the small puffed-rice cereal in a bowl. Pour over the toffee mixture and stir well to mix.

Step three Spoon into the tin and press flat. Leave in a cool place until quite firm and then cut into squares.

Be sure to use small puffed-rice cereal for this recipe. Larger puffed-rice grains absorb too much liquid.

Crunchy Top Lemon Cake

The same crunchy topping can be used on traybakes and teabreads.
The secret is to pour the crunchy topping over the cake while it is still
warm so that the lemon soaks in and the sugar stays on top.

Step one Preheat the oven to 180°C/fan 160°C/gas 4. Butter the
cake tin, then line the base with non-stick baking parchment.

Step two Measure all the ingredients for the cake into a large
bowl and beat for about 2 minutes or until smooth and well
blended. Turn the mixture into the prepared tin and level the
surface.

Step three Bake in the preheated oven for 35–40 minutes or
until the cake has shrunk slightly from the sides of the tin and
springs back when lightly pressed in the centre with a finger.

Step four While the cake is baking, make the crunchy topping.
Measure the lemon juice and sugar into a bowl and stir until
blended. When the cake comes out of the oven, spread the
lemon paste over the top while the cake is still hot. Leave
to cool completely in the tin, then turn out and peel off the
parchment. Serve with clotted cream or mascarpone cheese.

*If a softened cake has sunk disastrously in the middle, cut
this out, fill with softened fruits and whipped cream, and
serve as a dessert.*

Serves 6–8

**Cake tin needed:
a deep, round
18cm (7in) cake tin**

100g (4oz) butter,
softened

175g (6oz)
caster sugar

175g (6oz)
self-raising flour

1 level tsp
baking powder

2 large eggs, beaten

4 tbsp milk

finely grated zest
of 1 lemon

for the topping

juice of 1 lemon

100g (4oz) caster
or granulated sugar

Chocolate Rum Cake

This moist chocolate cake is laced with rum, then filled and covered with a glossy chocolate icing that melts in the mouth. It is irresistible to chocoholics, and can be served as an afternoon cake, or as a pudding with single cream.

Serves 8

Cake tin needed:
a deep, round 18cm (7in) cake tin

200g (7oz) plain chocolate (39 per cent cocoa solids)

100g (4oz) cubed unsalted butter

3 large eggs, separated

100g (4oz) dark muscovado sugar

50ml (2fl oz) dark rum

75g (3oz) sifted self-raising flour

50g (2oz) ground almonds

for the filling and icing

225g (8oz) plain chocolate (39 per cent cocoa solids)

100g (4oz) diced unsalted butter

4 level tbsp apricot jam

Step one Preheat the oven to 180°C/fan 160°C/gas 4. Butter the cake tin, then line the base with non-stick baking parchment.

Step two Break the chocolate into pieces and melt with the butter gently in a heatproof bowl set over a pan of barely simmering water or in a microwave, taking care not to burn the chocolate, stirring occasionally. Allow to cool slightly. Put the egg yolks and the sugar into a large bowl and whisk until pale and creamy. Add the cooled chocolate mixture and the rum and mix well. Gently fold in the flour and the ground almonds.

Step three In a separate bowl, whisk the egg whites until stiff but not dry, then lightly fold into the mixture. Turn into the tin and gently level the surface.

Step four Bake in the preheated oven for about 45 minutes or until well risen and the top of the cake springs back when lightly pressed in the centre with a finger. Leave to cool in the tin for a few minutes, then turn out, peel off the parchment and finish cooling on a wire rack.

Step five To make the filling and icing, melt the chocolate, as above. Add the diced butter and stir until the mixture has the consistency of thick pouring cream. Slice the cake in half horizontally and use a little icing to fill it. Warm the apricot jam, then push through a sieve. Brush this over the cake top and sides and allow to set. Smooth the icing over and leave to set.

For a video masterclass on icing a cake, go to
www.mykitchentable.co.uk/videos/icing

Strawberry Dessert Cake

This is absolutely delicious served warm with cream, when it tends to be more of a dessert. Served cold, it is more of a cake.

Step one Preheat the oven to 160°C/fan 140°C/gas 3. Butter the tin, and line the base with non-stick baking parchment.

Step two Measure the flour, baking powder and sugar into a bowl. In a separate bowl, beat the eggs and vanilla extract together, then stir them into the dry ingredients along with the melted butter. Stir until thoroughly mixed, then spread half the mixture in the prepared tin.

Step three Arrange the strawberries on top to within 1cm (½in) of the edge. Spoon the remaining mixture on top of the strawberries, then spread to cover the surface. It does not matter if there are a few gaps; the mixture will liquefy as it starts to bake in the heat of the oven and will spread to fill them. Sprinkle with almonds.

Step four Bake in the preheated oven for 1½ hours or until the cake is golden brown and shows signs of shrinking from the side of the tin. Leave to cool in the tin for 15 minutes, then turn out and peel off the baking parchment. Serve warm or cold, with cream.

The unbaked cake can be covered and kept in the fridge for up to 24 hours, but it will need time to come back up to room temperature before baking, following the recipe above.

This cake is easily adaptable. Try fresh, sliced peaches instead of strawberries and add almond extract instead of vanilla. It is also excellent with apples, but with these I add 1 tsp grated lemon zest rather than vanilla extract.

Serves 6–8

Cake tin needed:
a 20cm (8in) round, 5cm (2in) deep, loose-bottomed fluted flan tin or cake tin

225g (8oz)
self-raising flour

1½ **level tsp baking powder**

225g (8oz)
caster sugar

2 **large eggs**

1 tsp vanilla extract

150g (5oz)
butter, melted

350g (12oz) sliced
strawberries

25g (1oz) flaked
almonds

Lemon Swiss Roll

This recipe is delicious flavoured with orange, too. Substitute an orange for the lemon and orange marmalade for the lemon curd.

Serves 6–8

Cake tin needed:
a 33 x 23cm (13 x 9in) Swiss roll tin

4 large eggs

100g (4oz) caster sugar

finely grated zest of 1 lemon

100g (4oz) self-raising flour

for the filling

4 level tbsp lemon curd

Step one Preheat the oven to 220°C/fan 200°C/gas 7. Butter the tin, then line with non-stick baking parchment.

Step two Whisk the eggs, sugar and lemon zest in a large bowl until the mixture is light and frothy and the whisk leaves a trail when lifted out. Sift the flour into the mixture, carefully folding it in at the same time. Turn the mixture into the prepared tin and give it a gentle shake so that the mixture finds its own level, making sure that it spreads evenly into the corners.

Step three Bake in the preheated oven for about 10 minutes or until the sponge is golden brown and begins to shrink from the edges of the tin. While the cake is cooking, place a piece of non-stick baking parchment a little bigger than the size of the tin onto a work surface and sprinkle it with caster sugar.

Step four Invert the cake onto the sugared parchment. Quickly loosen the parchment on the bottom of the cake and peel it off. Trim the edges of the sponge with a sharp knife and make a score mark 2.5cm (1in) in from one shorter edge, being careful not to cut right through.

Step five Leave to cool slightly, then spread with the lemon curd. If the cake is too hot, the lemon curd will soak straight into the sponge. Roll up the cake firmly from the cut end.

Baked Apple Lemon Sponge

Something like the old fashioned Eve's Pudding, but this one makes its own creamy, lemon sauce. If buying lemon curd, check that it contains butter, sugar and lemons. It may be labelled lemon cheese or luxury lemon curd.

Step one Preheat the oven to 160°C/fan 140°C/gas 3. Place the heavy baking tray to heat in the oven.

Step two To prepare the base, measure the cream, lemon curd, sugar and flour into a bowl and beat until smooth. Slice the apples very thinly. (I find it easiest to use the thin slicing disc in the food processor or a mandolin cutter.) Mix the sliced apples into the cream mixture, spoon into the ovenproof dish and level with the back of a spoon.

Step three To make the topping, measure all the ingredients except the demerara sugar into a mixing bowl. Beat until smooth, then spread gently over the fruit in the ovenproof dish. Sprinkle with the demerara sugar.

Step four Bake in the preheated oven on the hot baking tray for 30 minutes or until a perfect golden brown.

Step five Cover the pudding with foil, then continue to bake for a further 45 minutes or until the sponge springs back when lightly pressed in the centre with a fingertip. Serve warm.

The unbaked pudding can be kept covered in the fridge for up to 6 hours. Bring up to room temperature before baking in the preheated oven on the hot baking tray.

Serves 6-8

**Equipment needed:
a heavy baking tray
a 27 x 18cm
(10½ x 7in) deep
ovenproof dish**

for the base
**300ml (½ pint)
single cream**

**6 level tbsp
lemon curd**

**2 level tbsp
caster sugar**

**1 heaped tsp plain
flour**

**750g (1¾lb)
cooking apples,
peeled and cored**

for the topping
2 large eggs

**175g (6oz)
self-raising flour**

**100g (4oz)
caster sugar**

**100g (4oz)
butter, softened**

**1 level tsp
baking powder**

2 tbsp milk

**1-1½ tbsp
demerara sugar**

Sticky Apricot Pudding

This is a very adaptable recipe and one of my family's favourites. You can use a variety of different fruits, either fresh or canned. It's a good dessert to serve for Sunday lunch. Just place the pudding on the top shelf, above the roast, and let it cook there. It couldn't be easier.

Serves 6–8

Equipment needed:
a 28cm (11in) shallow ovenproof baking dish

175g (6oz) self-raising flour

1 level tsp baking powder

50g (2oz) caster sugar

50g (2oz) butter, softened

1 large egg

grated zest of 1 lemon

150ml (¼ pint) milk

1 x 410g (14oz) tin apricot halves (or other tinned fruit), drained

for the topping

50g (2oz) butter, melted

175g (6oz) demerara sugar

Step one Preheat the oven to 230°C/fan 210°C/gas 8. Butter the ovenproof baking dish.

Step two Measure the flour, baking powder, sugar, butter, egg, lemon zest and milk into a large bowl. Beat together until the mixture forms a soft, cake-like consistency.

Step three Spread the mixture into the prepared baking dish and arrange the apricots, cut-side down, over the top. Brush or drizzle the melted butter for the topping over the apricots, then sprinkle with the demerara sugar.

Step four Bake in the preheated oven for 35 minutes or until the top has caramelised to a deep golden brown. Serve warm, with crème fraîche, whipped cream, ice cream or even hot custard on a cold winter's day.

You can replace the apricots with whatever fruit you have to hand. Both sliced dessert and cooking apples work well. Arrange the apple slices evenly over the top of the sponge mixture. Other good alternatives are rhubarb and plums. Cut the plums in half and remove the stones, then arrange them cut-side down.

Treacle Sponges

A great family favourite for a cold winter's day.

Step one Butter the pudding basins. Blend the syrup with the lemon juice and divide among the basins.

Step two Measure all the remaining ingredients into a mixing bowl and beat well for 2 minutes or until well blended. Divide the mixture among the basins and smooth the tops.

Step three Take four pieces of non-stick baking parchment, each large enough to cover the top and down the sides of a basin. Place a piece of foil of the same size on top of each piece of baking parchment. Form a pleat in all four pairs of paper and foil. Smooth one pleated paper and foil pair over each basin and down the sides, with the foil uppermost. Secure in place with some string. The pleat in the lid will allow for the expanding steam and pudding.

Step four Steam in a steamer, or place in a large pan with enough boiling water to come halfway up each basin, for 45 minutes (see tip, below). Turn out and serve with extra, warm golden syrup.

Keep the water boiling in the pan, topping up when needed with more boiling water. Stand the pudding basins on an old, upturned saucer to keep them off the pan bottom.

Makes 4

Equipment needed:
4 x 175ml (6fl oz)
pudding basins

8 tbsp golden syrup

1 tbsp lemon juice

grated zest of
1 lemon

100g (4oz) butter,
softened

100g (4oz)
caster sugar

2 large eggs

100g (4oz)
self-raising flour

1 level tsp
baking powder

warm golden
syrup, to serve

Passion Sponge

This is a variation of my ever-popular passion pudding. It takes all of five minutes to make.

Serves 4–6

an 18–20cm (7–8in) ready-made sponge flan case

400g (14oz) tin raspberries in natural juice

framboise or cassis liqueur (optional)

150ml (¼ pint) double cream (not extra thick)

225g (8oz) Greek-style yoghurt

1–2 tbsp light soft brown sugar

100g (4oz) fresh raspberries, to decorate

Step one Place the sponge flan case on a serving plate. Drain the raspberries, saving the juice, and spoon them evenly over the flan case. Spoon over a little of the reserved juice with a splash of the liqueur, if desired.

Step two Whisk the double cream until stiff, then fold in the Greek yoghurt. Pile it on top of the raspberries.

Step three Sprinkle over the sugar and chill until the sugar has melted into the topping. Decorate with fresh raspberries just before serving.

Apple and Mincemeat Steamed Pudding

The breadcrumbs give this pudding an extra-light texture.

Step one Butter the pudding basin. Measure the flour, suet and breadcrumbs into a bowl. Add sufficient milk to make a soft dough and then divide into three portions, in graded sizes.

Step two Roll out the smallest portion to line the base of the basin. Add half the mincemeat, apples and sugar, then roll out the second portion of pastry to fit over the fruit. Place the remaining fruit on top, then cover with the remaining pastry rolled out to fit the top of the basin.

Step three Take a piece of non-stick baking parchment large enough to cover the top and down the sides of the basin. Place a piece of foil of the same size on top of the baking parchment and form a pleat in the paper and foil together. Smooth this over the basin and down the sides, with the foil uppermost. The pleat in the lid will allow for the expanding steam and pudding. Secure in place with some string. Steam in a steamer, or place in a large pan with enough boiling water to come halfway up the basin (see tip, below), for about 3 hours. Turn out and serve with custard.

Keep the water boiling in the pan, topping up when needed with more boiling water. Stand the basin on an old, upturned saucer to keep it off the pan bottom.

Serves 6

Equipment needed:
a 1.2 litre (2 pint)
pudding basin

175g (6oz)
self-raising flour

115g (4oz)
shredded beef
or vegetarian suet

50g (2oz) fresh white
breadcrumbs

150ml (¼ pint) milk

225g (8oz) mincemeat

450g (1lb) cooking
apples, peeled,
cored and sliced

50g (2oz) light
muscovado sugar

custard, to serve

Guernsey Apple Cake

A wonderful way to use up some apples if you have a glut, this is best served warm with whipped cream. Expect it to dip a little in the middle.

Serves 6–8

Cake tin needed:
a deep, round 18cm (7in) cake tin

225g (8oz) self-raising brown flour

grated zest of 1 lemon

1 level tsp baking powder

100g (4oz) butter

225g (8oz) light muscovado sugar

2 large eggs

175g (6oz) apples, peeled, cored and chopped

icing sugar, for dusting

Step one Preheat the oven to 160°C/fan 140°C/gas 6. Butter the tin, then line the base with non-stick baking parchment.

Step two Measure the flour, lemon zest, baking powder, butter, sugar and eggs into a bowl and mix together until evenly blended and smooth. Fold in the chopped apples.

Step three Spoon the mixture into the prepared tin and bake for 1–1¼ hours or until well risen and the surface springs back when lightly pressed in the centre with a finger.

Step four Allow to cool in the tin for about 10 minutes before turning out to cool completely on a wire rack. Dust with icing sugar and eat within 1–2 days.

For Mary Berry's tips on how to line a baking tin, go to www.mykitchentable.co.uk/authors/MaryBerry/liningtins

English Muffins

These old-fashioned English muffins are traditionally pulled apart through the middle, not cut, and eaten warm with lashings of butter. Any left over will keep for 2–3 days in an airtight container and are then best split in half and eaten toasted.

Step one Flour the baking tray well. Measure the dry ingredients into a bowl or electric mixer, then pour in the milk in a continuous stream while mixing the ingredients, to form a dough. Knead the dough with your hands or with a mixer fitted with a dough hook until smooth and elastic.

Step two Turn the dough out onto a lightly floured work surface and roll out to a thickness of about 1cm (½in) with a floured rolling pin.

Step three Cut the dough into rounds using a 7.5cm (3in) plain cutter, place on the prepared tray and dust the tops with the semolina. Cover loosely and leave in a warm place until doubled in size (approximately 1 hour).

Step four Lightly oil the griddle or frying pan and place on the hob to heat. Cook the muffins, in 2–3 batches, for about 7 minutes each side, turning the heat down once the muffins go into the pan. When cooked, they should be well risen and brown on both sides. Cool slightly on a wire rack before splitting and buttering to serve.

Makes 14

Equipment needed:
a baking tray

a griddle or
heavy-based
frying pan

675g (1½lb)
strong white flour

2 level tsp
caster sugar

7g sachet
fast-action yeast

1½ level tsp salt

450ml (¾ pint)
tepid milk

1 level tsp fine
semolina, for dusting

oil, for lining the
griddle or pan

Orange Wholemeal Victoria Loaf

If you are making this loaf to give to a friend or to sell whole, use a loaf tin liner for a simple decorative touch.

Equipment needed:
a 900g (2lb) loaf tin

100g (4oz) butter, softened

100g (4oz) light muscovado sugar

2 large eggs

50g (2oz) wholemeal self-raising flour

50g (2oz) self-raising flour

grated zest of 1 orange

for the topping

25g (1oz) butter, softened

75g (3oz) sifted icing sugar

1 level tbsp fine-cut marmalade

Step one Preheat the oven to 180°C/fan 160°C/gas 4. Lightly butter the tin, then line the base with non-stick baking parchment, or use a 900g (2lb) loaf tin liner.

Step two Measure all the cake ingredients into a large bowl and beat well for about 2 minutes or until smooth and blended. Turn into the prepared tin and level the surface – don't expect the mixture to fill the tin.

Step three Bake in the preheated oven for about 40 minutes or until well risen, golden and shrinking slightly from the sides of the tin. Turn out onto a wire rack to cool.

Step four To make the topping, measure all the topping ingredients into a bowl and blend together until smooth. Spoon on top of the cold loaf and swirl the top with a small palette knife to decorate.

Honey-glazed Walnut Bread

This recipe makes very good bread, very quickly! It only needs mixing, shaping and rising once before baking, which takes as little as 1¼ hours. The recipe makes 16 rolls or two 20cm (8in) round loaves.

Step one Grease the trays. Briefly process the walnuts, or coarsely chop by hand, taking care to keep the pieces quite large. Set aside until ready to use.

Step two Measure the flours, yeast and salt into a large bowl and combine. Then add the treacle, milk and oil and mix, either with your hands or an electric mixer, to form a dough. Add a little more milk, if necessary, to make the dough slightly sticky. Turn the dough out onto a lightly floured work surface and knead for about 10 minutes. Alternatively, use a mixer fitted with a dough hook and leave running for about 5 minutes. When ready, the dough should be smooth and elastic and leave the bowl and your hands clean.

Step three Reserve about 2 tablespoons of the sunflower seeds, then work the rest, together with the chopped walnuts, into the dough. Shape the dough into 16 rolls, or divide the dough in half, and then shape each piece into a smooth round and set in the centre of the prepared baking trays. Enclose each tray inside a large plastic bag, sealing a little air inside so that the plastic is not in contact with the bread. Leave to rise in a warm place for 30–45 minutes or until doubled in size. If your kitchen is cool, this may take as long as 1–1½ hours.

Step four Preheat the oven to 200°C/fan 180°C/gas 6. To glaze the loaves, mix together the egg and honey and brush over the surface of the dough. Sprinkle with the reserved sunflower seeds, then bake in the preheated oven for 20–25 minutes or until the loaves are a good conker brown and sound hollow when tapped on the base. If you are making rolls remember that, as they are smaller, they will need less baking time in the oven. Cool on a wire rack.

Equipment needed:
2 baking trays

100g (4oz) walnut pieces

350g (12oz) granary flour

350g (12oz) strong white flour

7g sachet fast-action yeast

2 level tsp salt

1 tbsp black treacle

500ml (17fl oz) warm milk (1 part boiling to 2 parts cold)

2 tbsp good olive oil or walnut oil

100g (4oz) sunflower seeds

to glaze

1 tbsp beaten egg

1 tbsp clear honey

Walnut and Raisin Loaf

This generously fruited savoury loaf with added walnuts is delicious served with cheese.

Equipment needed:
a baking tray

225g (8oz) strong white flour

225g (8oz) strong wholemeal flour

1 level tsp salt

1 level tbsp light muscovado sugar

1 level tsp ground cinnamon

40g (1½ oz) butter, melted

7g (¼ oz) sachet fast-action yeast

100g (4oz) chopped walnuts

100g (4oz) raisins

extra flour, for dusting

1 large egg, beaten, to glaze

Step one Line the tray with non-stick baking parchment. Measure the flours, salt, sugar, cinnamon, butter, yeast and 300ml (½ pint) warm water into a bowl and mix together by hand or using an electric mixer fitted with a dough hook until combined to fairly sticky dough.

Step two Knead for 4–5 minutes on a lightly floured work surface or in the mixer, adding a little extra flour if needed.

Step three Transfer to a large oiled bowl, cover tightly with clingfilm (make sure no air can escape) and leave to rise in a warm place for 1–1½ hours or until the dough has doubled in size.

Step four Tip the dough onto a lightly floured work surface and flatten the ball slightly. Add the chopped walnuts and raisins and knead into the dough, then shape into a long thick sausage shape about 40 x 10cm (16 x 4in) or two smaller sausage shapes.

Step five Place on the prepared baking tray and slide into a large plastic bag, so the dough and the tray are completely covered. Seal the end of the bag. Leave in a warm place for 35–45 minutes or until doubled in size.

Step six Preheat the oven to 220°C/fan 200°C/gas 7. Brush the dough with beaten egg and bake in the preheated oven for 20–25 minutes for the large loaf (a little less for two smaller ones) or until golden brown and the bread sounds hollow when tapped on the bottom. Cool on a wire rack.

Irish Soda Bread

Soda bread is quick and easy to make, as it uses no yeast so does not have to rise. Porridge oats can be added to give the bread more texture. Simply replace 50g (2oz) of the flour with the same quantity of oats. Soda bread is best eaten on the day of making.

Step one Preheat the oven to 200°C/fan 180°C/gas 6. Lightly grease the tray.

Step two Measure the dry ingredients into a mixing bowl. Add the buttermilk (or milk and yoghurt mixture) and enough tepid water – about 6 tablespoons – to form a very soft dough.

Step three Turn the dough out onto a lightly floured work surface and shape into a neat round about 18cm (7in) in diameter. Place on the prepared baking tray and make a shallow cross in the top with a sharp knife.

Step four Bake in the preheated oven for 30 minutes, then turn the bread upside-down and continue baking for 10–15 minutes or until the bread sounds hollow when tapped on the bottom. Cool on a wire rack.

Equipment needed:
a baking tray

oil, for greasing

450g (1lb) strong white flour

1 level tsp bicarbonate of soda

1 level tsp salt

300ml (½ pint) buttermilk or 150ml (¼ pint) milk and 150ml (¼ pint) natural yoghurt, mixed

Crunchy Lemon Syrup Loaves

I've seen loaves similar to these for sale in Wycombe market. They may not look madly exciting, but they are very popular, and delicious.

Equipment needed:
2 x 450g (1lb) loaf tins

100g (4oz) butter, softened

175g (6oz) self-raising flour

1 level tsp baking powder

175g (6oz) caster sugar

2 large eggs

4 tbsp milk

finely grated zest of 1 lemon

for the topping

juice of 1 lemon

100g (4oz) sugar

Step one Preheat the oven to 180°C/fan 160°C/gas 4. Lightly butter the tins, then line the base of each with non-stick baking parchment.

Step two Measure all the loaf ingredients into a large bowl and beat well for about 2 minutes. Divide the mixture evenly between the tins and level the surface of each.

Step three Bake in the preheated oven for about 30 minutes or until the loaves spring back when lightly pressed in the centre with a finger.

Step four While the loaves are baking, make the crunchy topping. Measure the lemon juice and sugar into a small bowl and stir to mix. Spread the mixture over the baked loaves while they are still hot, and then leave to cool completely in the tins. Turn out and remove the parchment once cold.

Carrot and Orange Loaf

This moist loaf needs no buttering. Store it in the fridge, if you want to keep it for a length of time.

Step one Preheat the oven to 180°C/fan 160°C/gas 4. Lightly butter the tin, then line the base with non-stick baking parchment.

Step two Finely grate the zest from the orange, cut away the pith and slice the orange thinly. Set the slices aside and place the zest in a large bowl and add the butter, sugar, carrots, eggs, flour, baking powder and spice. Mix well until thoroughly blended. Add the tablespoon of milk, if necessary, to give a dropping consistency. Spoon into the prepared tin.

Step three Bake in the preheated oven for about 1 hour or until just firm to the touch. Remove the loaf from the oven and arrange the orange slices over the top. Brush with the honey and return the loaf to the oven for a further 15 minutes or until a skewer inserted into the centre comes out clean. Leave to cool in the tin for a few minutes, then turn out, peel off the parchment and finish cooling on a wire rack.

Equipment needed: a 900g (2lb) loaf tin

1 orange

150g (5oz) butter, softened

150g (5oz) light muscovado sugar

175g (6oz) carrots, grated

2 large eggs, beaten

200g (7oz) self-raising flour

1 level tsp baking powder

½ level tsp ground mixed spice

about 1 tbsp milk

to finish

about 2 tbsp clear honey

Walnut Teabread

This teabread freezes well. It's delicious spread with good butter, and I like coming across the walnuts – they give the bread an interesting texture.

Equipment needed:
a 900g (2lb) loaf tin

100g (4oz) sugar

175g (6oz)
golden syrup

200ml (7fl oz) milk

50g (2oz) sultanas

225g (8oz)
self-raising flour

1 level tsp
baking powder

50g (2oz) roughly
chopped walnuts

1 large egg, beaten

Step one Preheat the oven to 180°C/fan 160°C/gas 4. Lightly butter the tin, then line the base with non-stick baking parchment.

Step two Measure the sugar, syrup, milk and sultanas into a pan and heat gently until the sugar has dissolved. Set aside to cool.

Step three Measure the flour and baking powder into a bowl and add the roughly chopped walnuts. Add the cooled syrup mixture to the dry ingredients, along with the beaten egg, and stir well until the mixture is smooth. Pour into the prepared tin.

Step four Bake in the preheated oven for 50 minutes–1 hour or until firm to the touch and a skewer inserted into the centre comes out clean. Cover the top of the teabread loosely with kitchen foil towards the end of the cooking time, if the cake is becoming too brown. Leave to cool in the tin for 10 minutes, then turn out, peel off the parchment and finish cooling on a wire rack. Serve buttered.

To break up walnuts (or to pulverise biscuits or cornflakes), put them in a strong polythene bag and crush them with a rolling pin.

KITCHEN
TABLE

For Mary Berry's guide to ingredients, go to
www.mykitchentable.co.uk/authors/MaryBerry/ingredients

Cherry Loaf Cake

This loaf is always a favourite. Wash and dry the quartered cherries thoroughly to prevent them sinking to the bottom of the cake.

Step one Preheat the oven to 180°C/fan 160°C/gas 4. Butter the tin, then line the base with non-stick baking parchment.

Step two Put the quartered cherries into a sieve and rinse under running water. Drain well, then dry thoroughly on kitchen paper.

Step three Measure all the remaining ingredients into a large bowl and beat well for 1 minute to mix thoroughly. Lightly fold in the cherries. Turn into the prepared tin.

Step four Bake in the preheated oven for 1–1¼ hours or until risen well and golden brown, and a skewer inserted into the centre comes out clean. Leave to cool in the tin for 10 minutes, then turn out, peel off the parchment and finish cooling on a wire rack.

Equipment needed:
a 900g (2lb) loaf tin

175g (6oz) red or natural glacé cherries, cut into quarters

225g (8oz) self-raising flour

175g (6oz) butter, softened

175g (6oz) caster sugar

finely grated zest of 1 lemon

50g (2oz) ground almonds

3 large eggs

Danish Pastries

It's fiddly and time-consuming to make these pastries in their various traditional shapes, but they'll be better than any you can buy!

Makes 16

Equipment needed:
3 baking trays

for the pastry dough

450g (1lb) strong plain flour

½ level tsp salt

350g (12oz) butter, softened

7g sachet fast-action yeast

50g (2oz) caster sugar

150ml (¼ pint) warm milk

2 large eggs, beaten

225g (8oz) marzipan

a little beaten egg, for brushing

for the topping

100g (4oz) icing sugar

50g (2oz) toasted flaked almonds

Step one Butter the trays. Measure the flour and salt into a bowl and rub in 50g (2oz) of the butter. Add the yeast and sugar and stir. Make a well in the centre, add the warm milk and eggs, and mix to a soft dough. Knead until smooth, put into a clean bowl, cover with clingfilm and leave to rise in a warm place for about 1 hour or until the dough has doubled.

Step two Punch down the dough, and knead until smooth. Roll out to an oblong 35 x 20cm (14 x 8in). Dot pieces of butter over the top two-thirds of the oblong, using 150g (5oz) of the butter.

Step three Fold the bottom third up and the top third down. Seal the edges, then turn the dough so that the folded side is to the left. Roll out to an oblong, dot over the remaining butter and fold. Wrap in clingfilm and chill for about 15 minutes.

Step four Place the dough folded side to the left. Roll and fold it twice more. Wrap in clingfilm and chill for 15 minutes. Now, divide the dough into four equal pieces.

Step five Roll out each piece to a 40cm (16in) square, and then cut each into four squares. Put a piece of marzipan into the centre of each. Fold the corners in and press the edges down.

Step six Arrange the pastries on the trays, cover with oiled clingfilm and leave to prove for about 20 minutes in a warm place, until they are beginning to look puffy.

Step seven Preheat the oven to 220°C/fan 200°C/gas 7. Brush each pastry with a little beaten egg. Bake in the preheated oven for 15 minutes or until golden brown. Lift onto a wire rack. Make glacé icing by mixing 1–2 tablespoons warm water with the icing sugar. Trickle this over the pastries and sprinkle with almonds.

Classic Lemon Tart

A delicious tart with crisp sweet pastry and a sharp lemon filling.

Step one Make the pâte sucrée: measure the flour into a bowl and rub in the butter with your fingertips until the mixture resembles fine breadcrumbs. Stir in the sugar, then add the egg yolks and mix until the ingredients form a dough. Knead gently until smooth. Wrap the dough in clingfilm and leave to rest in the fridge for about 30 minutes.

Step two Remove the base from the tin and dust it and your work surface with flour. Place the dough ball in the centre of the base and flatten it out slightly. Roll out the pastry, still on the tin base, to 4cm (1½in) larger in diameter than the base.

Step three Lift the tin base off the work surface (use a palette knife to help you), supporting the pastry overhang as you do so. Drop the metal base into the tin, then ease the pastry into the edges and up the sides of the tin, slightly bending the overhang over the rim of the tin. If the pastry has cracked at all, simply press it together to seal. Press the pastry into the flutes of the tin, then lightly prick the pastry base (not quite all the way through) with a fork. Set on the baking sheet, cover loosely with clingfilm and chill for 30 minutes.

Step four Preheat the oven to 200°C/fan 180°C/gas 6. Remove the cling film and line the pastry with foil so it supports the sides and then fill with baking beans. Bake blind for 12-15 minutes, until the pastry is set, then lift out the foil and beans. Carefully trim the excess pastry from the sides using a sharp knife. Return the empty pastry case to the oven for another 10-12 minutes or until it is pale golden and completely dry. Set aside to cool. Reduce the oven temperature to 160C/Fan 140C/Gas 3.

Step five To make the filling, beat together the eggs, sugar, ground almonds and cream. Add the finely grated zest of all four lemons and the juice of two. Pour the filling into the pastry case and bake in the preheated oven for about 30-35 minutes or until just set but with a slight wobble in the centre. Leave to cool for a few minutes, then dust generously with icing sugar to serve.

Serves 6

Equipment needed:
23cm (9in)
loose-based
fluted tart tin
a baking sheet

for the pâte sucrée

175g (6oz) plain flour

75g (3oz) butter, softened

75g (3oz) caster sugar

3 large egg yolks

for the filling

2 large eggs

90g (3½ oz) caster sugar

150g (5oz) ground almonds

85ml (3½ fl oz) whipping or double cream (not extra thick)

4 lemons

to finish

icing sugar, for dusting

Glazed Fruit Tartlets

These little tarts look best when each one is filled with a single type of fruit. Use redcurrant glaze for red or dark blue fruits, but for orange or green fruits, such as green grapes and kiwi fruit, use apricot jelly for the glaze. Fill the pastry cases at the last moment as they soften quickly.

Makes 12

Equipment needed:
12-hole patty tin

for the pâte sucrée

100g (4oz) plain flour

50g (2oz) butter,
softened

50g (2oz) caster sugar

2 large egg yolks

for the filling and glaze

150ml (¼ pint) double cream (not extra thick)

225g (8oz) fresh fruits, such as raspberries, strawberries, or blackberries

about 4 tbsp
redcurrant jelly

Step one First, make the pâte sucrée (sweet pastry). Measure the flour into a bowl. Rub in the butter with your fingertips until the mixture resembles fine breadcrumbs. Stir in the sugar, then add the egg yolks and mix until the ingredients come together to form a dough. Knead the mixture gently until smooth. Wrap the dough in clingfilm and leave to rest in the fridge for about 30 minutes.

Step two Preheat the oven to 190°C/fan 170°C/gas 5. Roll out the pastry on a lightly floured work surface and cut out 12 rounds using a 7.5cm (3in) fluted pastry cutter. Re-roll the trimmings once only. Ease the pastry rounds into the holes in the patty tin and prick the bases lightly with a fork. Place a small piece of non-stick baking parchment or foil into each pastry case and fill with baking beans.

Step three Bake the pastry cases in the preheated oven for about 15 minutes or until golden brown. Turn out onto a wire rack, remove the paper or foil and baking beans, and leave to cool.

Step four To make the filling, whip the cream until it forms soft peaks and spoon a little into each tartlet case. Arrange the fruits on top. Warm the redcurrant jelly in a small pan and brush liberally over the fruits to glaze.

Tarte Tatin

This classic 'upside-down' French tart is usually served warm, as a pudding, rather than as a cold cake.

Step one First, prepare the pastry. Measure the flour, butter and icing sugar into a bowl and rub in the butter with your fingertips until the mixture resembles fine breadcrumbs. Add the egg yolk and enough water (about 1 scant tablespoon) to bring the mixture together to form a firm but not sticky dough. Knead lightly, wrap in clingfilm and chill for about 30 minutes.

Step two Preheat the oven to 200°C/fan 180°C/gas 6. Slice the apples and sprinkle with the lemon juice and zest. Measure the butter and sugar into a small pan and heat gently until the butter has melted and the sugar has dissolved. Pour into the base of the tin. Arrange a single layer of the best apples slices in a circular pattern over the mixture. Cover with the remainder of the apple slices.

Step three Roll out the chilled dough on a lightly floured work surface and use to cover the apples. Bake in the preheated oven for about 20 minutes or until the pastry is crisp and golden brown. It will have shrunk a little when cooked.

Step four Tip the juices from the tin into a small pan. Turn the tart out onto a plate, with the pastry on the bottom. Boil the juices to reduce to a syrupy caramel and pour over the apple. If there is very little juice – the amount will depend on the apples used – add 75g (3oz) demerara sugar to the pan with the juices and cook until syrupy. Serve warm, with cream, crème fraîche or yoghurt.

Serves 6

Cake tin needed:
a 23cm (9in)
sandwich tin

for the pastry

100g (4oz)
self-raising flour

50g (2oz) diced butter

1 level tbsp sifted
icing sugar

1 large egg yolk

for the topping

900g (2lb) eating
apples, peeled
and cored

finely grated zest
and juice of 1 lemon

75g (3oz) butter

75g (3oz)
demerara sugar

to finish

75g (3oz) demerara
sugar (optional)

Classic Apple Pie

This is one of my favourite desserts. I always decorate my sweet pies with a few pastry leaves, so that they look more inviting.

Serves 6

Equipment needed:
a shallow 900ml
(1½ pint) pie dish

675g (1½ lb) cooking
apples, peeled, cored
and thickly sliced

50–75g (2–3oz)
caster sugar,
depending on how
sweet or tart the
apples are

4 whole cloves

for the pastry

175g (6oz) plain flour

50g (2oz)
diced butter

50g (2oz) diced white
baking vegetable fat

milk, to glaze

sugar, for sprinkling

Step one Arrange half the apple slices in the bottom of the pie dish and sprinkle with the caster sugar. Arrange the cloves evenly among the apples. Cover with the remaining apple slices and add 3 tablespoons cold water.

Step two To make the pastry, measure the flour into a bowl. Add the diced butter and white vegetable fat and rub in with your fingertips until the mixture resembles fine breadcrumbs. Add about 2 tablespoons cold water and mix to a firm dough.

Step three Roll out the dough on a lightly floured work surface to a size that will cover the top of the pie dish. Lift the dough onto the dish and trim the edges. If you like, cut the trimmings into decorative shapes, such as leaves, and lightly press onto the dough. Chill in the fridge for 30 minutes.

Step four Preheat the oven to 200°C/fan 180°C/gas 6. Brush the pie with a little milk, then sprinkle the top with sugar. Make a small slit in the centre of the pie for the steam to escape. Bake in the preheated oven for 40–45 minutes or until the apples are tender and the pastry is crisp and pale golden. Cover the pie loosely with foil towards the end of the cooking time, if the pastry starts to brown before the apples are cooked.

You can freeze the pie after cooking and when completely cool. Leave to defrost almost completely before reheating and serving. Uncooked homemade pastry is an excellent standby for the freezer. Pack it in separate quantities of 225g (8oz) and 450g (1lb), labelling it clearly. Defrost in the fridge or kitchen until pliable enough to roll and use.

Frangipane Tartlets

Pâte sucrée is the classic French sweet pastry. I make mine in a bowl or in the food processor, which is easier than the traditional way, where the flour is sifted onto a work surface, and the other ingredients are placed into a well in the flour and worked together to a paste before the flour is gently worked in.

Step one First, make the pâte sucrée (sweet pastry). Measure the flour into a bowl. Rub in the butter with your fingertips until the mixture resembles fine breadcrumbs. Stir in the sugar, then add the egg yolks and mix until the ingredients come together to form a dough. Knead the mixture gently until smooth. Wrap the dough in clingfilm and leave to rest in the fridge for about 30 minutes.

Step two Preheat the oven to 190°C/fan 170°C/gas 5. Roll out the pastry on a lightly floured work surface and cut out 12 rounds using a 7.5cm (3in) plain pastry cutter. Re-roll the trimmings once only. Ease the pastry rounds into the holes in the patty tin and prick the bases lightly with a fork. Chill while you are making the frangipane.

Step three To make the frangipane, measure the butter and sugar into a bowl and beat together well until light and fluffy. Gradually beat in the egg, then stir in the ground almonds and almond extract. Fill the chilled tartlet cases with the frangipane and scatter the flaked almonds on top.

Step four Bake in the preheated oven for about 15 minutes or until the frangipane is golden and firm to the touch. Ease the tartlets out of the tins and onto a wire rack to cool.

Step five Sieve the apricot jam into a small pan and warm gently. Brush the tartlets with the apricot glaze and decorate the outside edge with a thin line of ground almonds, then leave the tartlets to cool completely.

Makes 12

Equipment needed:
12-hole patty tin

for the pâte sucrée

100g (4oz) plain flour

50g (2oz) butter, softened

50g (2oz) caster sugar

2 large egg yolks

for the frangipane

50g (2oz) butter, softened

50g (2oz) caster sugar

1 large egg, beaten

65g (2½ oz) ground almonds

a few drops almond extract

50g (2oz) flaked almonds

to finish

3 tbsp apricot jam

2 tbsp ground almonds

Deep Treacle Tart

This is a familiar option on pub dessert menus, and a popular choice among adults and children alike. It is delicious served with cream, ice cream or custard.

Serves 6

Equipment needed:
a heavy baking tray
a deep 18cm (7in)
loose-based
fluted flan tin

for the pastry

175g (6oz) plain flour

75g (3oz) butter

for the filling

350g (12oz)
golden syrup

about 200g (7oz)
fresh white or brown
breadcrumbs

grated zest and juice
of 2 large lemons

Step one First, make the pastry. Measure the flour into a large bowl and rub in the butter with your fingertips until the mixture resembles fine breadcrumbs. Add 2 tablespoons cold water, or enough to mix to a firm dough, then wrap in clingfilm and chill in the fridge for about 20 minutes.

Step two Preheat the oven to 200°C/fan 180°C/gas 6 and put the tray in the oven to heat up. Roll out the pastry thinly on a lightly floured work surface and use it to line the flan tin.

Step three To make the filling, heat the syrup in a large pan and stir in the breadcrumbs and the lemon zest and juice. If the mixture looks runny, add a few more breadcrumbs (the amount you need will depend on whether you use white or brown bread). Pour the syrup mixture into the pastry case and level the surface.

Step four Bake in the preheated oven, on the hot baking tray, for 10 minutes and then reduce the oven temperature to 180°C/fan 160°C/gas 4 and bake for a further 25–30 minutes or until the pastry is golden and the filling set. Leave to cool in the tin. Serve warm or cold.

For more recipes from My Kitchen Table, sign up for our newsletter at
www.mykitchentable.co.uk/newsletter

Chocolate Éclairs

These are sheer luxury and well worth making. Do not fill choux pastry items too long before serving as the pastry tends to go soggy.

Step one Preheat the oven to 220°C/fan 200°C/gas 7. Lightly butter the trays. To make the choux pastry, put the butter and 150ml (¼ pint) water into a small pan over low heat. Bring slowly to the boil. Remove from the heat, add the flour all at once and beat until a soft ball forms and leaves the side of the pan. Allow to cool slightly. Then add the eggs a little at a time, beating really well after each addition to give a smooth, shiny paste. It is easiest to use a hand-held electric mixer for this.

Step two Spoon the mixture into a large piping bag fitted with a 1cm (½in) plain nozzle. Pipe onto the prepared baking trays into éclair shapes, about 13–15cm (5–6in) long, leaving room for them to spread. Bake in the preheated oven for 10 minutes, then reduce the heat to 190°C/fan 170°C/gas 5 and bake for a further 20 minutes or until well risen and a deep golden brown. (Any pale, undercooked parts will become soggy once cool.)

Step three Remove the éclairs from the oven and split them down one side to allow the steam to escape. Leave to cool completely on a wire rack.

Step four Whip the cream until it is firm enough to pipe. Fill the cold éclairs with cream, using a piping bag fitted with a plain nozzle.

Step five To make the icing, break the chocolate into pieces and put into a heatproof bowl set over a pan of barely simmering water, taking care not to burn the chocolate, stirring occasionally. Add the butter and 2 tablespooons water to the melted chocolate. Stir occasionally until the chocolate and butter have melted. Remove from the heat and add the sifted icing sugar, beating well until smooth. Spoon the icing over the top of each éclair, then leave to set before serving.

Makes 12

Equipment needed:
2 baking trays

for the choux pastry

50g (2oz) diced butter

65g (2½ oz) sifted plain flour

2 large eggs, beaten

for the filling

300ml (½ pint) whipping cream

for the icing

50g (2oz) plain chocolate (39 per cent cocoa solids)

15g (½ oz) butter

75g (3oz) sifted icing sugar

Austrian Apricot and Almond Tart

This tart looks wonderful cooked because the top layer of pastry moulds itself around the apricot halves.

Serves 8

Equipment needed:
a heavy baking tray
a 25cm (10in) loose-based, deep fluted
flan tin

for the pastry

275g (10oz) plain flour

150g (5oz) sifted
icing sugar

150g (5oz) diced
chilled butter

1 large egg, beaten

for the filling

175g (6oz) grated
marzipan

800g (1¾lb) tinned
apricot halves in
natural juice, drained

Step one To make the pastry, measure the flour and icing sugar into a bowl. Rub in the butter until the mixture resembles breadcrumbs. Stir in the egg and bring together to form a dough. Form into a ball, seal in a plastic bag and chill for 30 minutes.

Step two Preheat the oven to 180°C/fan 160°C/gas 4. Put the tray in the oven to heat.

Step three Cut off a little less than half the pastry, wrap it in clingfilm and return it to the fridge. Roll out the larger piece to a circle about 5cm (2in) bigger than the flan tin.

Step four Line the base and sides of the flan tin with the pastry, then trim the excess from the top edge with a knife. Spread the grated marzipan evenly over the base. Dry the apricots on kitchen paper, then evenly space them on top of the almond paste, rounded-side up.

Step five Roll out any leftover trimmings with the remaining pastry to a circle big enough to fit the top of the flan tin. Using a little water, dampen the rim of the pastry in the flan tin and then lift the top circle of pastry into position. Trim off any excess pastry, then press the edges together so no juices can escape.

Step six Place in the preheated oven to bake on the hot baking tray for 30–35 minutes or until pale golden. Watch the pastry carefully. If it is browning too quickly, protect the edge with crumpled strips of foil.

You can prepare the tart ahead of time. Cover the uncooked tart in clingfilm and chill for up to 24 hours, but remove the tart from the fridge for about 20 minutes before baking.

Profiteroles

Choux pastry must be cooked until it is really firm and has turned a good straw colour. The profiteroles look wonderful piled up in a pyramid.

Step one Preheat the oven to 220°C/fan 200°C/gas 7. Lightly butter the trays. Place the butter and 150ml (¼ pint) water in a small pan. Melt the butter, then bring slowly to the boil. Remove from the heat, add all the flour and beat until a soft ball forms. Beat over the heat for a further minute.

Step two Cool slightly. Add the eggs a little at a time, beating well after each addition to give a smooth, shiny paste. Spoon the mixture into a piping bag with a 1cm (½in) plain nozzle. Pipe 20 small mounds, spaced well apart, on the baking trays.

Step three Bake in the preheated oven for 10 minutes, then reduce the oven temperature to 190°C/fan 170°C/gas 5. Cook for a further 10 minutes or until well risen and a deep golden brown. Remove from the oven and split open. For really dry centres, after splitting, return to the oven at 180°C/fan 160°C/gas 4 for a further 10 minutes. Cool completely on a wire rack.

Step four When they are cold, use a piping bag fitted with a plain nozzle to fill the profiteroles with a little whipped cream.

Step five To make the icing, melt the chocolate pieces in a heatproof bowl set over a pan of barely simmering water or in a microwave. Stir in the butter and 2 tablespoons water. Remove from the heat. Beat in the icing sugar until smooth. Dip each profiterole into the icing to coat the top, then leave to set.

To freeze uncooked, pipe shapes onto non-stick baking parchment lined with clingfilm and open freeze. When firm, freeze in freezer bags for up to 3 months. Cook from frozen, allowing a few extra minutes cooking time. Split baked choux pastry and cool before freezing. Store in rigid containers in the freezer for 3–6 months. Crisp up in a hot oven, then cool and fill.

Makes 20

Equipment needed:
2 baking trays

for the choux pastry

50g (2oz) butter

65g (2½ oz) sifted plain flour

2 large eggs, beaten

for the filling

300ml (½ pint) whipping or double cream (not extra thick), whipped

for the icing

50g (2oz) plain chocolate (39 per cent cocoa solids), broken into pieces

15g (½ oz) butter

75g (3oz) sifted icing sugar

French Apple Tart

This delicious tart is an economical choice in the autumn, when you can use your own apples or get them cheaply from elsewhere.

Serves 6

Equipment needed:
a deep 20cm (8in)
loose-based fluted
flan tin

for the pastry

175g (6oz) plain flour

75g (3oz) diced butter

1 large egg yolk

for the filling

50g (2oz) butter

900g (2lb) cooking
apples, peeled,
quartered, cored
and chopped

4 level tbsp
apricot jam

50g (2oz) caster sugar

grated zest of ½ lemon

225g (8oz) eating
apples, peeled,
quartered and cored

1–2 tbsp lemon juice

about 1 tsp caster
sugar, for sprinkling

for the glaze

4 level tbsp
apricot jam

Step one Measure the flour into a bowl, add the butter and rub in with your fingertips until the mixture resembles fine breadcrumbs. Add the egg yolk, stir into the flour mixture with a round-bladed knife, and bring the mixture to a dough, adding a little water, if necessary. Knead the pastry very lightly, then wrap in clingfilm and chill in the fridge for about 30 minutes.

Step two Preheat the oven to 200°C/fan 180°C/gas 6. For the filling, melt the butter in a pan and add the cooking apples and 2 tablespoons water. Cover and cook gently for 10–15 minutes or until it is mushy. Rub the mixture through a sieve into a clean pan, and add the jam, sugar and grated lemon zest. Cook over high heat, stirring, for 10–15 minutes until all the excess liquid has evaporated and the mixture is thick. Set aside to cool.

Step three Roll out the pastry thinly on a lightly floured work surface and use to line the tin. Cover with non-stick baking parchment and fill with baking beans. Bake blind for 10–15 minutes in the preheated oven, then remove the paper and beans and bake for a further 5 minutes or until the pastry at the base of the flan has dried out. Remove from the oven, but do not turn off the oven.

Step four Spoon the cooled apple purée into the tart case and level the surface. Slice the eating apple quarters very thinly. Arrange in neat overlapping circles over the apple purée, brush with the lemon juice and sprinkle with the caster sugar. Return the tart to the oven and bake for 25 minutes or until the pastry and the edges of the apples are lightly browned.

Step five To make the glaze, sieve the apricot jam into a small pan and heat gently until runny. Brush all over the top of the apples and pastry. Serve warm or cold.

Filo Apple Strudels

I've used ready made filo pastry in this recipe, for ease. Try to find the shorter packets of filo pastry so that you won't need to trim the pastry to size. Any leftover filo will keep in the fridge for two days. Alternatively, you can wrap it carefully, put it into the freezer immediately and use within a month.

Step one Preheat the oven to 200°C/fan 180°C/gas 6. Lightly butter the trays.

Step two To prepare the filling, mix together the apples, lemon juice, sugar, breadcrumbs, sultanas and cinnamon in a bowl.

Step three Unfold one sheet of filo pastry and brush liberally with melted butter. Spoon one-eighth of the apple mixture to cover the middle third of the longest edge of the pastry, leaving a small border. Fold in this border, then bring the two short sides over the apple to cover it. Roll the filled pastry over and over to form a neat strudel. Put it on one of the prepared baking trays, then repeat the process with the remaining seven pastry sheets and apple mixture.

Step four Brush the strudels with melted butter, then bake in the preheated oven for 15–20 minutes or until golden brown and crisp. Meanwhile, blend the caster sugar and 2 tablespoons water together in a small pan and heat gently until all the sugar has dissolved. Spoon the syrup over the warm strudels and dust with icing sugar to serve.

Makes 8

Equipment needed:
2 baking trays

for the filling

350g (12oz) peeled, cored and roughly chopped cooking apples

juice of ½ lemon

75g (3oz) demerara sugar

25g (1oz) fresh breadcrumbs

50g (2oz) sultanas

1 level tsp ground cinnamon

8 sheets filo pastry 18 x 33cm (7 x 13in)

100g (4oz) butter, melted

for the topping

2 tbsp caster sugar

icing sugar, for dusting

For Mary Berry's guide to ingredients, go to
www.mykitchentable.co.uk/authors/MaryBerry/ingredients

Pecan Pie

This is an all-American creation that is delicious served with coffee, or as a dessert served with cream or ice cream.

Serves 6

Equipment needed:
a 23cm (9in)
loose-based
fluted flan tin
a baking tray

**for the rich
shortcrust pastry**

175g (6oz) plain flour

15g (½oz) icing sugar

75g (3oz) diced butter

1 large egg yolk

for the filling

25g (1oz) butter,
softened

175g (6oz) light
muscovado sugar

3 large eggs

200ml (7fl oz)
maple syrup

1 tsp vanilla extract

150g (5oz)
pecan halves

Step one To make the pastry, measure the flour and icing sugar into a large bowl and rub in the butter with your fingertips until the mixture resembles fine breadcrumbs.

Step two Add the egg yolk and 1 tablespoon cold water and mix until it comes together to form a firm dough. Wrap in clingfilm and leave to rest in the fridge for about 30 minutes. Preheat the oven to 200°C/fan 180°C/gas 6.

Step three Roll out the dough on a lightly floured work surface and use to line the tin. Prick the pastry all over with a fork, line with non-stick baking parchment or foil and fill with baking beans. Bake blind in the preheated oven for 15 minutes. Remove the baking beans and paper or foil and return the pastry case to the oven for 5 minutes or until it is pale golden and dried out. Remove from the oven and reduce the temperature to 180°C/fan 160°C/gas 4.

Step four To make the filling, beat the butter with the sugar. Add the eggs, maple syrup and vanilla extract and beat well.

Step five Put the tin on the baking tray, arrange the pecan halves over the pastry flat-side down, then pour in the filling. Bake in the preheated oven at the reduced temperature for 30–35 minutes or until set. The filling will rise up in the oven, but will fall back on cooling. Leave to cool, then serve warm with cream or ice cream.

Lemon Meringue Pie

This recipe uses an easy, quick crumb crust rather than the usual pastry base, and the filling does not have to be cooked before it goes into the pie. You have only to stir a few ingredients together and it is ready.

Step one Preheat the oven to 190°C/fan 170°C/gas 5.

Step two Put the biscuits into a plastic bag and crush with a rolling pin. Melt the butter in a medium-sized pan. Remove the pan from the heat and stir in the biscuit crumbs. Press into the bottom and up the sides of the flan dish and leave to set.

Step three Pour the condensed milk into a bowl, then beat in the egg yolks, lemon zest and strained lemon juice. The mixture will seem to thicken on standing, then loosen again as soon as it is stirred. This is caused by the combination of condensed milk and lemon juice and is nothing to worry about. Pour the mixture into the biscuit-lined dish.

Step four Whisk the egg whites until stiff but not dry. Gradually add the sugar, a teaspoon at a time, whisking well between each addition. Whisk until very stiff and all of the sugar has been added.

Step five Pile separate spoonfuls of meringue over the surface of the filling, then spread gently to cover the filling to the biscuit edge, lightly swirling the meringue.

Step six Bake in the preheated oven for 15–20 minutes or until the meringue is light brown. Leave to cool for about 30 minutes before serving warm.

The flan dish can be lined with the biscuit crumb mix, covered and kept in the fridge for up to 3 days. The filling can be mixed, covered and kept in the fridge for up to 8 hours before baking. Once baked, the pie can be eaten warm or cold, but the meringue shrinks a little on standing.

Serves 6

Equipment needed:
a deep 20cm (8in)
fluted flan dish

for the base

175g (6oz)
digestive biscuits

75g (3oz) butter

for the filling

1 x 397g (14oz) tin full-fat condensed milk

3 large egg yolks

finely grated zest
and juice of 3 lemons

for the topping

3 large egg whites

175g (6oz) caster
sugar

Banoffi Pie

The combination of toffee, banana and cream makes this one of the most popular desserts around. Make sure you use a non-stick pan for the toffee and watch it very closely while you are making it, as it can burn easily.

Serves 6

Equipment needed: a deep 23cm (9in) loose-based fluted flan tin

for the base

175g (6oz) ginger biscuits

65g (2½ oz) butter

for the toffee filling

100g (4oz) butter

100g (4oz) light muscovado sugar

2 x 397g (14oz) tins full- fat condensed milk

for the topping

300ml (½ pint) double cream (not extra thick)

1 large banana

a little lemon juice

a little grated Belgian milk or plain chocolate (39 per cent cocoa solids), for sprinkling

Step one To make the base, put the ginger biscuits into a polythene bag and crush them to crumbs with a rolling pin. Melt the butter in a small pan, remove from the heat and stir in the crushed biscuits. Mix well, then spread the mixture over the base and sides of the flan tin. Press the mixture with the back of a metal spoon and leave to set.

Step two To make the toffee filling, measure the butter and sugar into a large non-stick pan. Heat gently until the butter has melted and the sugar has dissolved, then add the condensed milk. Stir continuously and evenly with a flat-ended wooden spoon for about 5 minutes or until the mixture is thick and has turned a golden toffee colour. Take care – it burns easily! Turn it into the prepared crumb crust and leave to cool and set.

Step three To make the topping, whip the double cream until it just holds its shape, then spread it evenly over the cold toffee mixture. Peel and slice the banana and dip into a little lemon juice to prevent it discolouring. Pile the banana slices onto the middle of the cream and sprinkle the whole pie with grated chocolate. Remove the flan ring and transfer to a flat plate. Serve well chilled.

Most tins of condensed milk now have ring pulls, so the old method of simmering the tin in a pan of water for 4 hours to caramelise the condensed milk is not advised. You can, however, buy condensed milk that has already been caramelised, known as caramel condensed milk.

My Mother's Bread and Butter Pudding

This is a great family favourite as a pudding to follow a weekend lunch.
You can use semi-skimmed milk for a healthier pudding, or slices of
brioche instead of sliced white bread to make it even richer. Use a
rectangular dish so the bread fits better.

Step one Butter the ovenproof dish with a little of the melted
butter. Measure the dried fruit, sugar, lemon zest and spice
into a bowl and toss to mix well. Cut each slice of bread into
three strips.

Step two Take enough bread strips to cover the base of the
dish and dip one side of each strip in melted butter. Lay them
in the prepared dish, buttered-side down. Sprinkle with half
the dried fruit mixture. Repeat the layering, laying the bread
strips buttered-side up, and sprinkle with the remaining dried
fruit mixture. Lay the third and final layer of bread strips on top,
buttered-side up.

Step three Beat together the eggs and milk and pour over the
pudding. Sprinkle with demerara sugar, then leave to stand for
about 1 hour, if time allows. Meanwhile, preheat the oven
to 180°C/fan 160°C/gas 4.

Step four Bake in the preheated oven for about 40 minutes
or until the top is golden brown and crisp and the pudding
slightly puffed up. Serve hot, though there are some who
insist that it is just as delicious cold.

*You can prepare the pudding ahead of time and keep it
covered in the fridge for up to 6 hours before baking. Don't
sprinkle over the demerara sugar topping until 1 hour before
you are ready to bake.*

Serves 6–8

Equipment needed:
a deep 18 x 23cm
(7 x 9in)
ovenproof dish

100g (4oz)
butter, melted

250g (9oz) currants
and sultanas

75g (3oz) caster sugar

grated zest of 1 lemon

½ level tsp ground
mixed spice

12 thin slices white
bread, crusts removed

3 large eggs

600ml (1 pint)
full-fat milk

2 tbsp demerara
sugar, for sprinkling

Easy Lemon Cheesecake

An excellent, quick cheesecake that's always popular with my family.

Serves 8

Equipment needed:
a 23cm (9in) flan dish

for the base

10 digestive biscuits

50g (2oz) butter

25g (1oz)
demerara sugar

**for the cheesecake
filling**

150ml (¼ pint)
single cream

1 x 397g (14oz) tin full-
fat condensed milk

175g (6oz) low-fat
soft cheese

grated zest and juice
of 3 large lemons

fresh strawberries,
hulled and halved, to
decorate

Step one Put the biscuits into a plastic bag and crush with a rolling pin. Melt the butter in a medium-sized pan. Remove the pan from the heat and stir in the biscuit crumbs and sugar. Press evenly over the base and sides of the flan dish, then leave to set.

Step two To make the cheesecake filling, mix together the cream, condensed milk, soft cheese and lemon zest, then add the lemon juice a little at a time, whisking until the mixture thickens.

Step three Pour the mixture into the flan case and leave to chill in the fridge for 3–4 hours or overnight. Decorate with a few fresh, hulled and halved strawberries.

Continental Cheesecake

For this cooked cheesecake, use frozen mixed summer fruits, if fresh are unavailable. If the centre dips a little on cooling, it holds the fruit perfectly!

Step one Preheat the oven to 160°C/fan 140°C/gas 3. Lightly butter the tin and line the base with non-stick baking parchment.

Step two Put the biscuits into a plastic bag and crush with a rolling pin. Melt the butter in a medium-sized pan. Remove the pan from the heat and stir in the biscuit crumbs and sugar. Press into and up the sides of the prepared tin and leave to set.

Step three To make the cheesecake filling, measure the butter, sugar, curd cheese or ricotta, flour, lemon zest and juice, and egg yolks into a large bowl. Beat until smooth. Fold in the lightly whipped cream. Whisk the egg whites stiffly, then fold into the mixture. Pour onto the biscuit crust.

Step four Bake in the preheated oven for about 1½ hours or until set. Turn off the oven and leave the cheesecake in the oven for a further hour to cool. Run a knife around the edge of the tin to loosen the cheesecake, then push the base up through the cake tin.

Step five To make the topping, cook the red and black currants and blackberries (if using) in 2 tablespoons water in a pan and sweeten to taste. When the fruit has softened and released its juices, remove from the heat.

Step six Blend the arrowroot with 2 tablespoons cold water and add to the cooked fruit and liquid in the pan. Allow to thicken, then leave to cool. Stir the raspberries and strawberries (if using) into the other fruits, then pile on top of the cheesecake, levelling out evenly.

Serves 12

Cake tin needed: a 23cm (9in) loose-based cake tin

for the base

100g (4oz) digestive biscuits

50g (2oz) butter

40g (1½ oz) demerara sugar

for the filling

65g (2½ oz) butter, softened

225g (8oz) caster sugar

550g (1¼ lb) curd cheese or ricotta

40g (1½ oz) plain flour

finely grated zest and juice of 2 lemons

4 large eggs, separated

200ml (7fl oz) whipping or double cream (not extra thick), lightly whipped

for the topping

450g (1lb) mixed red currants, black currants, blackberries, strawberries or raspberries,

caster sugar, to taste

1 level tsp arrowroot

Apricot and Almond Meringue Gâteau

A lovely, delicately flavoured meringue, this is perfect for a very special dinner party. In season, you could use fresh apricots (stone about 350g/12oz, then cook and purée), but save and quarter a few for decoration.

Serves 6

Equipment needed:
2 baking trays

4 large egg whites

225g (8oz)
caster sugar

75g (3oz)
ground almonds

for the filling and sauce

100g (4oz)
ready-to-eat
dried apricots

a strip of lemon zest

100g (4oz) sugar

juice of ½ lemon

300ml (½ pint) double cream (not extra thick)

to finish

about 150ml (¼ pint)
whipping or double
cream (not extra
thick), whipped
(optional)

2 large, ready-to-eat
apricots, quartered, to
decorate (optional)

icing sugar, for dusting

Step one Preheat the oven to 140°C/fan 120°C/gas 1. Line the trays with non-stick baking parchment.

Step two Whisk the egg whites until stiff. Add the sugar, a teaspoonful at a time, whisking well between each addition. Whisk until the mixture is very stiff, stands in peaks, and all the sugar has been added. Fold in the ground almonds. Divide the mixture between the prepared baking trays and spread gently into two rounds that are 20cm (8in) in diameter.

Step three Bake in the preheated oven for 1–1¼ hours or until the baking parchment peels away from the base of the meringue (this meringue mixture is quite sticky so don't worry if it sticks a little in the middle). Leave the meringues to cool on a wire rack.

Step four To make the filling, put the apricots in a small pan with the strip of lemon zest and 150ml (¼ pint) water. Heat gently for about 20 minutes or until the apricots are very tender. Transfer to a food processor or blender and process until smooth. In a small pan, add the sugar and 150ml (¼ pint) water. Heat until the sugar has dissolved, then add the lemon juice and boil for 3 minutes to make a sugar syrup.

Step five Whip the cream until it holds its shape, and flavour with about one-third of the apricot purée. Use to sandwich the meringues together. If you like, you can decorate with the gâteau with rosettes of the whipped cream, topped with a quartered apricot, if using. Dust the top of the gâteau with icing sugar. Dilute the remaining apricot purée with the sugar syrup and serve as a sauce.

Strawberry Meringue Nests

Ordinary meringue could be used for these nests, but they won't be quite so firm, nor will they keep so well. Meringue cuite is traditional because it holds its shape so well and is drier. Vary the fruit in these nests depending on the season.

Step one Preheat the oven to 140°C/fan 120°C/gas 1. Line the tray with non-stick baking parchment.

Step two Put the egg whites into a large bowl and whisk until foaming. Sift the icing sugar through a fine sieve into the egg whites. Set the bowl over a pan of gently simmering water and whisk the whites and sugar together until very thick and holding their shape. Add the vanilla extract, if using, and whisk again to mix. Be careful not to let the bowl get too hot or the meringue mixture will crust around the edges.

Step three Spoon the mixture into a piping bag fitted with a large star nozzle. Pipe six basket shapes onto the prepared baking tray, starting at the centre and then building up the sides of each basket.

Step four Bake in the preheated oven for about 45 minutes or until crisp and dry. Carefully lift off the tray and allow to cool on a wire rack.

Step five Halve the strawberries, if large, and use to fill the cold nests. Warm the redcurrant jelly in a small pan and gently spoon over the strawberries to glaze.

To make Baby Meringues, follow the ingredients and recipe for Meringue Nests, then pipe the mixture into 30 tiny shapes such as baskets, shells, spiral oblongs and fingers. Bake in the preheated oven until crisp and dry and then carefully lift off the baking trays onto a wire rack to cool.

Makes 6

Equipment needed:
a baking tray

for the meringue cuite

4 large egg whites

240g (8½oz)
icing sugar

a few drops vanilla
extract (optional)

for the filling

225g (8oz)
strawberries

about 2 tbsp
redcurrant jelly

Crème Brûlée

This baked creamy custard tastes like sheer luxury, but is easy to make. Choose an individual dish or a shallow dish that will withstand being put under the grill. If you overcook the mixture, it will form bubbles.

Serves 6–8

Equipment needed:
a 900ml (1½ pint)
shallow ovenproof dish
or 6–8 small ramekins
a roasting tin

4 large egg yolks

25g (1oz) caster
sugar and a few drops
vanilla extract, or 25g
(1oz) vanilla sugar
(see tip, below)

300ml (½ pint) single
cream and 300ml
(½ pint) double cream
(not extra thick)

about 50g (2oz)
demerara sugar

Step one Preheat the oven to 160°C/fan 140°C/gas 3. Butter the ovenproof dish or the ramekins.

Step two Beat the egg yolks with the caster sugar and vanilla extract, or the vanilla sugar. Heat the creams to scalding point (just too hot to put your finger in), leave to cool slightly, then add to the egg yolks in a steady stream, beating all the time. Pour into the dish or ramekins.

Step three Stand the dish or ramekins in the roasting tin half-filled with hot water. Bake in the preheated oven for 45 minutes or until set for the single dish, 25–30 minutes for the ramekins. Remove from the oven and leave to cool. Cover, then chill in the fridge overnight. These can be made up to two days ahead.

Step four Preheat the grill to hot. Sprinkle the top of the custard with demerara sugar to about 5mm (¼in) thickness and place under the grill, on a high shelf, until the sugar melts then caramelises to a golden brown–about 3–4 minutes. Keep a careful watch to make sure the sugar does not burn. Or use a cook's blowtorch, if you have one.

Step five Leave to cool, then chill for 2–3 hours before serving. Chilling again after caramelising gives time for the topping to become slightly less hard, and makes it easier to crack and serve. If you leave it much longer, the caramel melts and softens, which is not as attractive and does not taste as good.

Vanilla sugar adds a wonderful flavour. Simply store two or three vanilla pods in a jar of caster sugar. After about two weeks, the sugar is imbued with the pungency of the vanilla.

Apricot and Orange Cheesecake

The powdered gelatine needed for this recipe is easy to use, provided you soak it in cold water to form a sponge first.

Step one Put the biscuits into a sturdy plastic bag and crush with a rolling pin. Melt the butter in a medium-sized pan. Remove the pan from the heat and stir in the biscuit crumbs and sugar. Press into the cake tin and leave to set.

Step two Place 4 tablespoons water in a small bowl, sprinkle the gelatine and leave to 'sponge'. Place the apricots in a pan with the orange juice, bring to the boil, then simmer gently for about 5 minutes or until the apricots are tender.

Step three Tip the apricots into a food processor and add the honey, cream cheese, soured cream and egg yolks. Process until well mixed and smooth. Alternatively, you can push the apricots through a nylon sieve, then mix with the honey, cream cheese, soured cream and egg yolks with a wooden spoon.

Step four Set the bowl of gelatine over a pan of gently simmering water and allow to dissolve. Mix into the apricot mixture. Whisk the egg whites until frothy, add the caster sugar a little at a time, whisking well after each addition. Whisk until all the sugar has been added and the mixture is very stiff. Turn the mixture into the apricot mixture and fold well together.

Step five Pour the mixture onto the biscuit crust and chill in the fridge to set. Loosen the edges of the tin, using a small palette knife, if necessary. Push up the base of the tin and slide the cheesecake onto a serving plate.

Step six Heat the apricot jam, push it through a sieve and spread it over the cheesecake. Place 10 ratafia biscuits around the edge of the top of the cheesecake and serve chilled.

Serves 10

Cake tin needed:
a 23cm (9in)
loose-based cake tin

100g (4oz) digestive or oat biscuits

50g (2oz) butter

25g (1oz) demerara sugar

for the cheesecake

15g (½ oz) packet powdered gelatine

175g (6oz) ready-to-eat dried apricots

200ml (7fl oz) fresh orange juice

3 tbsp clear honey

225g (8oz) full fat cream cheese

150ml (¼ pint) soured cream

2 large eggs, separated

100g (4oz) caster sugar

for the topping

2 tbsp apricot jam

10 small ratafia biscuits

Pineapple and Ginger Fool

This is simplicity itself. Serve in attractive glasses or a large serving dish.

Serves 4

400g (14oz) tin crushed pineapple, drained

4 pieces stem ginger, drained and chopped

450ml (¾ pint) Greek-style yoghurt

toasted almond flakes, to sprinkle

4 mint sprigs, to decorate

Step one Mix together the pineapple, stem ginger and Greek-style yoghurt.

Step two Pour into glasses or a large bowl and chill thoroughly before serving, sprinkled with almonds and decorated with sprigs of fresh mint.

Coffee and Banana Vacherin

Use half caster sugar and half light muscovado sugar, if you prefer a less caramel-flavoured meringue.

Step one Preheat the oven to 140°C/fan 120°C/gas 1. Line the trays with non-stick baking parchment and mark each with a 20cm (8in) circle.

Step two Whisk the egg whites until stiff. Add the sugar, a teaspoonful at a time, whisking well between each addition, until the mixture is very stiff, stands in peaks, and all the sugar has been added.

Step three Spoon the meringue mixture into a large piping bag fitted with a 1cm (½in) plain nozzle. Pipe the meringue out to fill the circles on the baking parchment, piping in a spiral pattern, starting at the centre.

Step four Bake in the preheated oven for 1–1¼ hours or until the meringues are crisp and dry and lightly coloured. Allow to cool in the oven and then peel off the parchment.

Step five To make the filling, whip the cream until it holds its shape, and flavour with the dissolved coffee granules. Slice the bananas thinly and fold into the cream, making sure they are well coated to prevent discoloration. Spread over one meringue circle, and then place the other circle on top. Dust lightly with sifted icing sugar and decorate with rosettes of whipped cream.

You can make the meringue circles the day before, but don't keep the filled cake for too long, as the bananas will eventually turn brown.

Serves 6

Equipment needed:
2 baking trays

4 large egg whites

225g (8oz) light muscovado sugar

for the filling

300ml (½ pint) double cream (not extra thick)

1 level tsp instant coffee granules, dissolved in a little water

2 ripe bananas

to finish

sifted icing sugar, for dusting

150ml (¼ pint) whipping or double cream (not extra thick), whipped

Brandy Chocolate Charlotte

This is very rich so the slices should be quite small. The loaf shape is easy to serve. You'll need to prepare this a day in advance.

Serves 8

Equipment needed: a 900g (2lb) loaf tin

about 20 sponge fingers (boudoir biscuits)

3 tbsp brandy

for the mousse

100g (4oz) plain chocolate (39 per cent cocoa solids)

2 large eggs

175g (6oz) unsalted butter, softened

150g (5oz) caster sugar

to decorate

150ml (¼ pint) whipping cream

grated chocolate

Step one First, line the tin with non-stick baking parchment. Dip 8–9 sponge fingers sugar-side down in the brandy and arrange sugar-side down on the base of the tin.

Step two Cut the remaining sponge fingers in half and dip sugar-side down in the brandy. Stand them sugar-side out around the inside edge of the tin.

Step three Make the mousse by breaking the chocolate into pieces and placing in a heatproof bowl set over a pan of barely simmering water, or in a microwave, taking care not to burn the chocolate. Allow it to melt slowly. Put the melted chocolate, eggs, butter and sugar in a food processor and blend until smooth. Alternatively, beat well with a whisk. Turn into the loaf tin and smooth the top. Chill overnight.

Step four The next day, turn out onto a serving dish. Whisk the cream until thick, then pipe rosettes on the charlotte. Decorate with the grated chocolate.

Tiramisu Cake

Look out for the soft Italian sponge fingers called savoiardi, which are available from good delicatessens, to replace the trifle sponges. This dessert freezes well.

Step one Line the tin with non-stick baking parchment. Dissolve the coffee in the boiling water and mix with the brandy.

Step two Break the eggs into a bowl, add the sugar and whisk together at high speed until thick and frothy – the mixture should leave its own trail when trickled from a height. Blend a little of this mixture with the mascarpone in another bowl, then stir in the remaining egg and sugar mixture.

Step three Whisk the cream until thick and fold into the egg and mascarpone mixture. Coarsely chop the chocolate chips in a food processor to give chocolate bits and powder.

Step four Split the sponge fingers and line the prepared tin with half of them. Sprinkle over half the coffee mixture and scatter over one-third of the chocolate, then add half the mascarpone mixture. Add a second layer of sponge, then the remaining coffee mixture and another third of the chocolate.

Step five Cover with the rest of the mascarpone mixture and sprinkle with the remaining chocolate. Chill for four hours, then turn out of the tin, remove the parchment and serve very cold.

Serves 8

Cake tin needed: a round 20–23cm (8–9in) loose-based springform cake tin

1 generous tsp instant coffee granules

120ml (4fl oz) boiling water

85ml (3fl oz) brandy

2 large eggs

65g (2½ oz) caster sugar

250g (9oz) mascarpone cheese

300ml (½ pint) double cream (not extra thick)

75g (3oz) chocolate chips

1 packet trifle sponges

Baked Alaska

This is impressive to serve but surprisingly easy to make. It makes a good alternative style of birthday cake, decorated with sparklers.

for the sponge

Equipment needed:
a 23cm (9in)
sandwich tin
a large ovenproof
serving dish

2 large eggs

75g (3oz) caster sugar

50g (2oz)
self-raising flour

for the filling

1 tbsp sherry
(optional)

225g (8oz)
strawberries

1 litre (1¾ pints)
strawberry ice cream

**for the meringue
topping**

4 large egg whites

225g (8oz)
caster sugar

50g (2oz) flaked
almonds, for
sprinkling

icing sugar,
for dusting (optional)

Step one Preheat the oven to 190°C/fan 170°C/gas 5. Lightly butter the tin and line the base with non-stick baking parchment.

Step two To make the sponge, place the eggs and sugar in a large bowl. Beat at full speed with an electric whisk until pale in colour and thick enough to just leave a trail when the whisk is lifted. Sift the flour over the surface of the mixture and gently fold in with a metal spoon or spatula. Turn into the prepared tin and tilt the tin to allow the mixture to spread evenly to the sides.

Step three Bake in the preheated oven for 20–25 minutes or until springy to the touch and beginning to shrink from the sides of the tin. Turn out and leave on a wire rack until cold.

Step four Place the sponge on an ovenproof serving dish, sprinkle it with the sherry, if using, then scatter with the strawberries, leaving a small gap around the edge. Slice the ice cream and arrange it in a dome shape over the strawberries. Put into the freezer while you make the meringue.

Step five Preheat the oven to 230°C/fan 210°C/gas 8. To make the meringue, whisk the egg whites at full speed until stiff but not dry. Add the sugar, a teaspoonful at a time, whisking at high speed between each addition. Whisk until all the sugar has been added and the meringue is thick and glossy.

Step six Take the cake and ice cream from the freezer. Pile the meringue over the top and sides, ensuring the ice cream and sponge are all covered. Sprinkle over the flaked almonds, then bake immediately in the oven for 3–4 minutes or until well browned. Dust with icing sugar, if using, and serve immediately.

Ginger Cream Roll

This is a no-cook pudding, but I've included it here because it is such an easy but impressive-looking pudding to make. It does have to be made a day before serving to allow the brandy, biscuits and cream to meld together. Serve at a winter dinner party.

Step one Measure half the whipping cream into a bowl and whisk until it forms fairly stiff peaks. Quickly dip each biscuit in a little brandy, then sandwich together with the cream, shaping the sandwiched biscuits into a long roll. Place on a serving dish, cover and leave in the fridge overnight.

Step two The next day, whip the remaining cream and use it to cover the roll completely. (If you like, you can pipe rosettes down the length of the roll using a piping bag.) Decorate with slices of stem ginger. To serve, cut the roll into diagonal slices.

To fill a piping bag, stand the bag with the nozzle pointing down into a jug and then fold the top edges of the bag over the top of the jug. That way, it is much easier to spoon the whipped cream into the bag without getting it all over yourself. If you don't have a piping bag, you can use two plastic food bags put inside each other for strength and cut off one corner to create a funnel.

Equipment needed:
a long serving dish

450ml (¾ pint)
whipping cream

225g (8oz)
ginger biscuits

4 tbsp brandy

stem ginger slices,
to decorate

Hot Lemon Soufflé Pudding

This is one of my favourite lemon puddings. I have even baked it ahead of time and reheated it very satisfactorily, in a roasting tin of water for 30 minutes in a moderate oven. The top of the pudding is a spongy mousse, while underneath is a sharp lemon sauce.

Serves 4–6

Equipment needed:
a shallow 1.5 litre
(2½ pint) ovenproof
dish

a roasting tin

75g (3oz) butter,
softened

250g (9oz)
caster sugar

3 large eggs,
separated

75g (3oz)
self-raising flour

grated zest and
juice of 2 lemons

450ml (¾ pint) milk

Step one Preheat the oven to 190°C/fan 170°C/gas 5. Butter the ovenproof dish.

Step two Measure the butter and caster sugar into a bowl and beat until smooth. Beat in the egg yolks, then beat in the flour, lemon zest, juice and milk. Do not worry if the mixture looks curdled at this stage – this is quite normal.

Step three In another bowl, whisk the egg whites until they form soft peaks then carefully fold them into the lemon mixture using a large metal spoon.

Step four Pour the mixture into the prepared ovenproof dish and place in the tin. Pour enough boiling water into the tin to come halfway up the ovenproof dish and bake in the preheated oven for 1 hour or until pale golden brown on top.

Buy thin-skinned lemons that feel heavy for their size. To get maximum juice from them, it helps if the fruit is warm, or at least at room temperature. Before grating the zest, wash and dry the fruit well. Grate the zest on the small-holed side of the grater, and remember to scrape everything off the back of the grater after grating. A pastry brush is a useful tool to do this.

Hot Chocolate Soufflés

Soufflés like this are not difficult to make, but take care with the timing.

Step one Preheat the oven to 190°C/fan 170°C/gas 5 and place a baking sheet in it. Butter the individual soufflé dishes or the large soufflé dish. Break the chocolate into pieces and place in a pan along with 2 tablespoons water and 2 tablespoons of the milk. Stir over a low heat until the chocolate has melted, then add the remaining milk and bring to the boil. Remove the pan from the heat.

Step two Melt the butter in a small pan, stir in the flour and cook on a low heat for 2 minutes without browning, stirring continuously. Remove from the heat and stir in the hot chocolate milk, return to the heat and bring to the boil, stirring until thickened. Add the vanilla extract and leave to cool.

Step three Beat the egg yolks, one at a time, into the cooled chocolate sauce, then sprinkle over the sugar. In another bowl, whisk the egg whites until stiff but not dry. Stir one tablespoon into the mixture, then carefully fold in the remainder.

Step four Pour into the individual soufflé dishes or large soufflé dish, run a teaspoon round the edge and bake on the hot baking sheet in the preheated oven for 10 minutes for the individual soufflés or about 40 minutes for the large soufflé. Dust with icing sugar and serve with whipped cream, if using.

To make Orange Soufflés, omit the chocolate and the 2 tablespoons of water in step one, and add the finely grated zest of two small oranges and the juice of half an orange to the milk. Also omit the vanilla extract and increase the caster sugar to 75g (3oz).

If you are serving a soufflé for a supper party, make the sauce base ahead of time, including the addition of the yolks and flavourings. Then, 40 minutes before baking and serving, fold in the whisked egg whites, turn into the dish and bake.

Serves 4

Equipment needed: 4 x 225ml (8fl oz) individual soufflé dishes or a 1.2 litre (2 pint) soufflé dish

a baking sheet

100g (4oz) plain chocolate (39 per cent cocoa solids)

300ml (½ pint) milk

40g (1½ oz) butter

40g (1½ oz) plain flour

¼ tsp vanilla extract

4 large eggs, separated

50g (2oz) caster sugar

sifted icing sugar, for dusting

whipped cream, to serve (optional)

Crème Caramel

Cook Crème Caramel very slowly so the custard does not boil, which makes the crème tough and full of holes. Serve it very cold.

Serves 6

Equipment needed:
6 small ramekins or a
1 litre (1¾ pint)
soufflé dish

a roasting tin

for the caramel

155g (4oz) sugar

for the crème

6 large eggs

50g (2oz) caster sugar

few drop
vanilla extract

700ml (1¼ pints) milk

Step one Preheat the oven to 150°C/fan 130°C/gas 2. Make the caramel by placing the sugar and 3 tablespoons water in a heavy-based pan. Dissolve the sugar, stirring occasionally, over a low heat. When it has dissolved, bring to the boil, without stirring. Boil rapidly until the syrup is a pale golden brown. Remove from the heat and quickly pour the caramel into the small ramekins or the soufflé dish.

Step two Make the crème by mixing together the eggs, sugar and vanilla extract. Warm the milk in a pan until it is just hand-hot, then pour it into the egg mixture, stirring lightly.

Step three Butter the sides of the ramekins or dish above the caramel. Strain the crème through a fine sieve into the ramekins or dish. Place in a roasting tin half-filled with hot water.

Step four Bake the crème in the ramekins for about 45 minutes or in the soufflé dish for about 1 hour or until a knife inserted in the centre comes out clean. Do not worry if it takes longer than the time given to cook. It will set eventually. Do not increase the oven temperature or the crème will have bubbles in it.

Step five Remove from the oven and leave to cool completely for at least 12 hours or overnight in the fridge. Turn out carefully onto a flat dish or dishes sufficiently deep to catch the caramel juices.

Do not attempt to make caramel in a pan that is non-stick or has a dark interior. You cannot see clearly when the caramel is dark enough, and I have found it impossible to make a caramel in a non-stick pan. The syrup crystallises and will not caramelise. Heavy-gauge aluminium or stainless-steel pans are best.

Orange Jaffa Cheesecake

A very smooth, fresh cheesecake – the ginger biscuits go really well with the orange. This is the easiest cheesecake to make, but you'll need to leave about 30 minutes for the jelly to almost set.

Step one Lightly butter the cake tin.

Step two Mix together the ingredients for the base and spread over the bottom of the prepared tin, pressing down firmly.

Step three Dissolve the jelly in 150ml (¼ pint) boiling water, then add the orange juice to make it up to 300ml (½ pint). Put in a cold place until the jelly is thick and nearly set.

Step four Mix the cream cheese with the sugar and the almost-set jelly and then fold in the whipped cream. Turn into the tin on top of the biscuit crumbs and put in a cool place to set.

Step five To serve, loosen the sides of the cheesecake from the tin and push up the base, or remove the sides of the springform tin and slide the cheesecake onto a plate. Decorate with thinly sliced strips of orange zest.

Serves 8

Cake tin needed:
a 20cm (8in) round
loose-based or
springform cake tin

for the base

50g (2oz)
butter, melted

100g (4oz) ginger
biscuits, crushed

25g (1oz)
demerara sugar

for the cheesecake

600ml (1 pint)
packet orange jelly

150ml (¼ pint)
Jaffa orange juice

350g (12oz) full-fat
cream cheese

100g (4oz)
caster sugar

150ml (¼ pint)
whipping
cream, whipped

orange zest strips,
thinly sliced, to
decorate

Basic White Meringues

Meringues are easily broken, so store them in a rigid airtight tin or plastic container, with kitchen paper in between them. Meringues should be creamy in colour, not ice-white, or else they look as though they were bought in a shop. If you use golden caster sugar, expect darker meringues – they will taste just as good.

Makes 18

Equipment needed:
2 baking trays

3 large egg whites

175g (6oz)
caster sugar

for the filling

300ml (½ pint)
whipping or double
cream (not extra
thick), whipped

icing sugar, for
dusting (optional)

Step one Preheat the oven to 120°C/fan 100°C/gas ½. Line the trays with non-stick baking parchment.

Step two Put the egg whites in a large bowl and whisk until stiff but not dry. Add the sugar, a teaspoonful at a time, whisking well after each addition until all the sugar has been added. The meringue should be stiff and glossy.

Step three Fit a 1cm (½in) plain nozzle onto a large nylon piping bag and stand, nozzle down, in a large measuring jug. Spoon the meringue into the bag. Squeeze the meringue mixture towards the nozzle and twist the top of the piping bag to seal. Pipe the meringue into 18 'shells' 5cm (2in) in diameter on the prepared baking trays. Alternatively, use a pair of dessertspoons to shape the mixture into 18 mini meringues.

Step four Bake in the preheated oven for 1–1½ hours or until they are a creamy colour and can be lifted easily from the baking parchment without sticking. Turn off the oven, set the door ajar and leave the meringues until cold. Serve them sandwiched with whipped cream and dusted with icing sugar, if you like.

To make Brown Sugar Meringues, follow the recipe above but instead of 175g (6oz) caster sugar, use half light muscovado sugar and half caster sugar.

Index

10 9 8 7 6 5 4 3 2 1

Published in 2011 by Ebury Press, an imprint of Ebury Publishing. A Random House Group company

This edition published in 2013 for Index Books

Recipes © Mary Berry 2011
Book design © Woodlands Books Ltd 2011
Photography by William Reavell © Woodlands Books Ltd (see also credits below)

All recipes contained in this book first appeared in *Mary Berry's Quick and Easy Cakes* (1993), *Mary Berry's Ultimate Cake Book* (1994), *Mary Berry Cooks Puddings and Desserts* (1997), *Mary Berry Cooks Cakes* (1998) and *Mary Berry Foolproof Cakes* (2004). Mary Berry has asserted her right to be identified as the author of this Work in accordance with the Copyright, Designs and Patents Act 1988.

Mary Berry has asserted her right to be identified as the author of this Work in accordance with the Copyright, Designs and Patents Act 1988

All rights reserved. No part of this publication may be reproduced, stored in a retrieval system, or transmitted in any form or by any means, electronic, mechanical, photocopying, recording or otherwise, without the prior permission of the copyright owner.

The Random House Group Limited
Reg. No. 954009

Addresses for companies within the Random House Group can be found at www.randomhouse.co.uk

A CIP catalogue record for this book is available from the British Library

The Random House Group Limited supports The Forest Stewardship Council® (FSC®), the leading international forest certification organisation. Our books carrying the FSC label are printed on FSC® certified paper. FSC is the only forest certification scheme endorsed by the leading environmental organisations, including Greenpeace. Our paper procurement policy can be found at www.randomhouse.co.uk/environment

To buy books by your favourite authors and register for offers visit www.randomhouse.co.uk

Printed and bound in India by Replika Press Pvt. Ltd.

Colour origination by AltaImage

Commissioning Editor: Muna Reyal
Project Editor: Constance Novis
Designer: Lucy Stephens
Food Stylist: Katie Giovanni
Copy Editor: Emily Hatchwell
Production: Rebecca Jones

Photography on pages 10, 53, 165, 169, 205 © Jean Cazals; 14, 17, 18, 26, 34, 42, 50, 54, 77, 114, 154, 161, 162, 170, 198 © Dan Jones; 113, 146, 166,181, 186, 197 by Philip Webb © Woodlands Books Ltd

ISBN: 978 1 849 90336 3